Theodore F. Adams

Tell Me How

Theodore F. Adams

Tell Me How

HARPER & ROW, PUBLISHERS

New York, Evanston, and London

TO

TEDDE, LEIGH ANN, TRIP,
TED III, LESLIE, and MARK

who will be asking and answering
questions for a long time

Contents

	Foreword	*ix*
1.	Please Tell Me How . . .	*1*
2.	How to Face Up to Life	*11*
3.	How to Look at Yourself	*21*
4.	How to Become More than You Are	*27*
5.	How to Be Good and Good for Something	*35*
6.	How to Be Like a Tree	*43*
7.	How to Practice What You Preach	*49*
8.	How to Know the Supreme Fact in Life	*56*
9.	How to Live a New Kind of Life	*66*
10.	How to Become a Better Christian	*76*
11.	How to Be Found Faithful with Life	*82*
12.	How to Live in Peace	*92*
13.	How the Lord Helps Those Who Help Themselves	*98*
14.	How Prayer Can Mean More to You	*106*
15.	How the Bible Can Mean More to You	*116*
16.	How to Live in the Space Age	*125*
	Notes	*133*

Foreword

THE TWO INCIDENTS CITED in the opening chapter provide the theme and basis for this book. They reinforce a statement I heard a lecturer make some years ago: "There is no real learning except in answer to questions already in the listener's mind." Sometimes we help most by first stating the question and then seeking an answer in the Word of God, in the riches of human experience, and in the resources of Christian faith and life.

The members of the church family it is my privilege to serve have through the years helped me both by asking and answering questions and by encouraging me to do so. They have taught me a great deal concerning how to preach and how to live. To them I voice my appreciation and affection.

I am also grateful to my secretary, Emma Hutchins, for her patience in transcribing the manuscript, and to Charles L. Wallis for his friendly encouragement and invaluable editorial assistance.

I trust that the chapters in this volume will help some readers to find answers to questions already in their minds and will stimulate further search for insight and understanding of the Word of God and the way of life made so real in "the Word. . . made flesh" who "dwelt among us. . . full of grace and truth."

THEODORE F. ADAMS

First Baptist Church
Richmond, Virginia

Tell Me How

1.

Please Tell Me How...

A YOUNG WOMAN, WHO is a member of the church I serve, once told me that she missed something in my week-by-week preaching. I had asked for her comments, and so I welcomed her willingness to speak without qualms or hesitation. "You preachers are forever telling us what to do," she said, "but you seldom tell us how to do the things you preach about. *Please tell me how.*"

This reminded me of something one of my own children had once said: "Daddy, you don't ask enough questions in your sermons. Why don't you ask the questions that are in our minds? *Then tell us how to find the answers.*"

Long ago a man whom we call—perhaps undeservedly—"Doubting Thomas" said to Jesus, "Lord, we know not whither thou goest; and how can we know the way?" Jesus replied, "I am the way" (John 14: 5-6).

The requests of my parishioner and of my son prompted the writing of the chapters of this book, which finds its impetus, centrality, and purpose in the words of Christ, "I am the way." My thoughts in these pages concern the questions people most frequently ask me on *how* a happier and more dynamic Christian life may be achieved.

1

In this introductory chapter I turn to those topics which seem most persistently to be on the minds of Christians. How to worship, how to pray, how to read the Bible, how to grow as a Christian, and how to face the future—nearly every counseling period or pastoral visit inevitably turns to one or more of these aspects of the Christian life.

Elsewhere in this book most of these topics will be handled in greater detail. For the moment, however, I wish to consider each in capsule form—or as a pump primer for the pages that follow.

I

However frequently we attend church, most of us realize that there are more blessings to be gained from worship than we have discovered. Hence the repeated request. "Please tell me how to worship."

The key to a fuller understanding and appreciation of worship is found in the words Jesus spoke to the woman who at midday had gone to Jacob's well near Sychar, "God is a Spirit: and they that worship him must worship him in spirit and in truth" (John 4:24). This Samaritan woman had argued that her people believed God should be worshiped on their holy place, Mount Gerizim—whose peak towered in the distance—and that Jesus' people preferred Mount Zion. Jesus told her that true worship did not involve geography nor chronology. Rather, true worship is a matter of spirit.

When we possess the proper spirit, we can worship God anywhere, although, of course, some places are more conducive to worship than others. Surely this proper spirit is something we need to acquire. Wishing to publish a picture-story of a typical service of worship, a mass-circulation magazine dispatched a photographer to a typical church. The photographer took ten pictures of the worshiping congregation during the pastoral prayer, but not one of the photographs could be published. In each picture at least one individual was looking up or gazing at other persons when he should have had his head bowed reverently in prayer.

Three words suggest ways by which we may more truly worship. The first word is *preparation*. Before a service of worship we need properly to prepare our own hearts. "Prepare to meet thy God"

(Amos 4:12) is a worthy admonition for those who enter the sanctuary. To prepare ourselves by prayer at home is far more spiritually beneficial than to put on the proper Sunday-go-to-meeting clothes. Pray for the minister that God's message may be mediated through him. Expect to receive a blessing, and you will. Approach the Throne of Grace with an open mind and an eager heart.

The second word is *participation*. Be in your place of worship on time or better still, ahead of time. Join in the singing of hymns and the reading of responses. Pray with the pastor. Listen attentively and thoughtfully as he shares God's Word with you. Common worship requires a certain give-and-take between pastor and people. Resist the temptation to be passive or to sit back and say, "Well, I wonder if he will say anything worth listening to." When you pray for him and think with him, you will receive new insights into God's truth and guidance for your own personal needs.

The third word is *proclamation*. Worship does not conclude with the benediction. Worship, rather, culminates in the translation of the Word into loving, saving deeds. We leave worship empowered to witness to others of what we have seen, heard, felt, and experienced in the sanctuary. One man worshiped profitably, for he returned to his home and wrote in his diary. "The minister preached a good sermon, and I applied it to myself."

II

I have known church members who have participated—perhaps only perfunctorily—in public worship for many years. Yet in the midst of some excruciating crisis, they discover that they do not know how to pray. They push the panic button and find that the battery is dead. Or prayer for them is a dull thing, lacking in luster and in the sense of spiritual adventure. They listen to the familiar words:

> Prayer is the soul's sincere desire,
>   Uttered or unexpressed;
> The motion of a hidden fire,
>   That trembles in the breast.[1]

But these words do not ring true in their experience. Or when they pray they never really feel God's presence, sometimes doubt if he actually cares, and wonder if prayer is anything more than simple autosuggestion.

Even the disciples, who presumably had each been reared in pious Jewish homes, who had been taught according to the curriculum of the synagogue school, and who then shared a rich and intimate companionship with Jesus, knew that something was lacking in their prayers. "Lord," they beseeched him, "teach us to pray" (Luke 11:1). Hence the repeated request, "Please tell me how to pray."

Regularity is prerequisite to meaningful prayer. Jesus commended persistent prayer in his parables of the midnight caller (Luke 11:5-8) and of the importuning widow (Luke 18:1-8). We need to set apart specific periods for the cultivation of holy desires, to talk with God, and to link our lives with the Infinite. Morning and evening prayers bring a rich harvest of the spirit. God is always close to us, and in a moment, in the turning of a thought, whatever the situation or occasion, we may talk with him in prayer.

We should pray in faith, believing that God hears our prayers and that no worthy human interest or desire is beyond the range of his love. In the home of a church member who is totally deaf, I carried on my part of the conversation by writing on pieces of paper. Then he asked, "Will you pray for me?" As we bowed our heads, I wondered at first how the prayer could be effective? Then I realized anew that we were praying to God. That pastoral call became one of the golden moments in my life, for I realized as never before that primarily prayer is talking with God and to him alone. Jesus said, "When thou prayest, enter into thy closet, and when thou hast shut thy door, pray to thy Father which is in secret" (Matt. 6:6). At nighttime a little boy, who customarily said his prayers aloud, knelt by his bed, but he said nothing. When he got up, his mother asked why he hadn't prayed. He said he had. "But I didn't hear you." To which the boy replied, "But, mother, this time I wasn't talking to you."

Pray in anticipation that God will bring to pass a change within you by emptying you of your helplessness, greed, sin, and guilt, thereby making it possible for his life, will, and purpose to enter your life.

> Lord, what a change within us one short hour
> Spent in Thy presence will prevail to make!
> What heavy burdens from our bosoms take,

> What parched grounds refresh as with a shower!
> We kneel, and all around us seems to lower;
> We rise, and all, the distant and the near,
> Stands forth in sunny outline brave and clear;
> We kneel, how weak! we rise, how full of power![2]

But prayer, like worship, is not an isolated spiritual experience. We rise from prayer, but the prayer continues as we live the way we pray. We cannot find God in prayer and then lose him after we have said amen. We cannot surrender our lives to him in prayer and then claim to be independent of his will. We cannot pray for all God's children and then harbor ill will and animosity toward others. Prayer is ineffectual in a vacuum. Coleridge rightly perceived this when he wrote:

> He prayeth well who loveth well
> Both man and bird and beast.
> He prayeth best who loveth best
> All things both great and small;
> For the dear God who loveth us,
> He made and loveth all.[3]

III

Every level of our lives has felt the influence of the Bible. From no other source has come such enlightenment, guidance, and hope. Supremely, the Bible is for Christians the Word of Life in which we find him who is the Word Incarnate. Whether we read or neglect the Bible, none of us would question the significance of this Book for goodness and progress both personal and social. Hence the repeated request, "Please tell me how to read the Bible."

The inspiration received from the Bible differs with the reader, but no inspiration is without value. There are varieties of helpful ways to read the Bible, but it is more important that the Bible be read. The Bible does not mean the same thing to everyone, but we should permit it to mean all that by the grace of God is possible. Renewal of life and reinvigoration of faith accompany every searching of the pages of the Word for truth and power.

In the language of a gifted writer, Henry van Dyke has given us words which correctly interpret much that the Bible has meant to the believer:

Born in the East and clothed in Oriental form and imagery, the Bible walks the ways of all the world with familiar feet and enters land after land to find its own everywhere.

It has learned to speak in hundreds of languages to the heart of man.

It comes into the palace to tell the monarch that he is a servant of the Most High, and into the cottage to assure the peasant that he is a son of God.

Children listen to its stories with wonder and delight, and wise men ponder them as parables of life.

It has a word for the time of peril, a word of comfort for the time of calamity, a word of light for the hour of darkness.

Its oracles are repeated in the assembly of the people, and its counsels whispered in the ear of the lonely. The wicked and the proud tremble at its warnings, but to the wounded and penitent it has a mother's voice.

The wilderness and the solitary place have been made glad by it, and the fire on the hearth has lit the reading of its well-worn pages.

It has woven itself into our dearest dreams, so that love, friendship, sympathy and devotion, memory and hope, put on the beautiful garments of its treasured speech, breathing of frankincense and myrrh.

No man is poor or desolate who has this treasure for his own.[4]

Although I shall defer to a later chapter the giving of more fully developed ideas on this question, let me at this point make three suggestions which have proven helpful to many in reading the Bible.

First, as you have opportunity—and ought we not to make the opportunity?—read and become acquainted with the *whole* Bible. Admittedly there are some portions that are difficult reading, clothed in a language and symbolism that are strange to us, full of detailed genealogies and legalisms, but these generally are of minor consequence and somewhat apart from the glowing message of our eternal salvation. To know the whole Bible and something of the background of each of its books is to understand more fully the everlasting plan of God, the books Jesus knew and so frequently quoted, and the culmination of the age-old messianic expectation in Bethlehem and on Golgotha. When we read in snatches and by fits and starts, preferring a few priceless though isolated passages and cling to a handful of "proof texts," then we limit ourselves to a half-dozen rooms in a sixty-six-room mansion.

Secondly, become familiar with biblical language and thought. "I store thy word within my heart, to keep myself from sinning against thee" (Ps. 119:11, MOFFATT). This familiarity will be a reservoir of inspiration, beauty, help, and guidance that will shore up your weak will, irresolution, timidity, and despair in times of trouble, discouragement, and testing. Dr. John A. Redhead, a distinguished Southern preacher, recalls that in a low and desperate period of his life he got a lift which has sustained him ever since by remembering this one verse: "My God shall supply all your need according to his riches in glory by Christ Jesus" (Phil. 5:19). In the midst of a hectic situation a New York businessman found new hope and assurance just when he needed it most when words learned as a child became for him a spiritual oasis: "Now the Lord of peace himself give you peace always by all means" (2 Thess. 3:16).

Thirdly, secure copies of the more recent versions of the Bible. Although nothing will ever take the place of the beloved King James Version in the minds of many persons, old verses will live again and shine with new meaning as you read familiar truths phrased in the language and idiom of our generation.

IV

We begin our Christian lives, as Paul says, as "babes in Christ" (1 Cor. 3:1). Growth as a Christian is neither spontaneous nor automatic. "For the earth bringeth forth fruit of herself; first the blade, then the ear, after that the full corn in the ear" (Mark 4:28). Christian growth calls for persistent practice as we seek to move from one plateau of knowledge and faith to the next. Hence the repeated request, "Please tell me how to grow as a Christian."

We must be willing to *receive.* Receptivity is sometimes particularly difficult for the new believer. His heart is overflowing with a radiant experience. He is likely to be a religious activist, and this must not be unduly discouraged. However, we should remember that God required the Hebrew slaves to remain in the wilderness for forty years before he bestowed upon them the privilege of freedom. After his baptism, our Lord went into the wilderness for forty days that he might meditate and commune with God and so gird his mind for his divine mission. And following his conversion, the Apostle Paul sought out the quiet and repose of a distant sanctuary.

We surely require for growth those periods when we give little or nothing but are vessels which God may fill with his word and spirit.

We need those times when he will lead us "beside the still waters" (Ps. 23:2) so that our souls may be restored. "Be still, and know that I am God" (Ps. 46:10). We should be responsive to every prompting and urging of the Bible, to the permeating influences of regular worship, and to the instruction and challenge of those whose rewarding experience may strengthen our feeble faith.

We must be willing to *give*. We could not—and should not if we could—retain to ourselves all that we receive. "Freely ye have received, freely give" (Matt. 10:8). Louis Ginsberg has wisely written:

> The only things we ever keep
> Are what we give away.[5]

In one of Margaret Lee Runbeck's novels a woman named Amoret says to the women in her church group:

> "We'll start a little hospital in the town. . . . Our church treasury is beginning to be very respectable now. . . . We can't use the money just for the church . . . we must begin helping the town with it."

And another character, Opal, replies:

> "I reckon a church is jest like a human. . . . It learns to take care of itself first, and then it learns to take care of other people."[6]

Our giving should follow a predetermined and systematic pattern and not just as the mood strikes us or from our leftovers. The first book in the Old Testament commends the tithe as a reasonable expression of our appreciation of God's prodigality toward us and our responsibility to the work of his Kingdom. Throughout the centuries this standard has been recommended by the church. To set aside at least one-tenth of one's income for the Lord increases mightily the joys of Christian discipleship.

You must also be willing to *serve*. We can hardly expect to grow as Christians if we are unwilling to dedicate, not only our money, but also our time and talents. Indeed, to write a check may be an easy escape for those who are too selfish to recognize that both purses and persons are needed. Every Christian has some place where his particular abilities will count for Christ and the church. Not all of us can blaze trails in pioneer missionary endeavor or render some spectacular public service. Some are needed to keep bright the lights of home. The Apostle Paul knew that men were enabled to undertake various services in Christ's vineyard: "His 'gifts unto men' were varied. Some he made his messengers, some prophets, some preachers of the Gospel; to some he gave the power to guide and teach his people. His gifts were made that Christians might be properly equipped for their service, that the whole body might be built up until the time comes when, in the unity of common faith and common knowledge of the Son of God, we arrive at real maturity—that measure of development which is meant by 'the fullness of Christ' " (Eph. 4:11-13, PHILLIPS). Blind Milton with keen insight wrote:

They also serve who only stand and wait.[7]

In the novel, *An Episode of Sparrows,* David Wix thinks of all the little children who romp in the less-attractive streets of London, and he says with an assumed piety, "Remember, not one sparrow can fall to the ground—" To this Olivia gives a vigorous rejoiner:

"But they fall all the time. . . . We knock them down. We knock them, crush them—carelessly or carefully, it doesn't matter which, and they fall. That's what humans do to humans, so don't talk to me about God. . . . Wait," she said. "Humans to humans? . . . Is that how it works? Someone, one person at least, is meant to see the fall and care? . . . See and become the instrument. I have seen. I wish I hadn't . . . but I have and I shall keep my eyes open."[8]

His eye is on the sparrow—and so should ours be. "I beseech you therefore, brethren . . . that ye present your bodies a living sacrifice, holy, acceptable unto God, which is your reasonable service" (Rom. 12:1).

V

The world in which we are now living has been variously described as in flux, in revolution, in a period of readjustment, and in perpetual crisis. It seems improbable that we shall know peace in our time. Always we are aware that the pressing of a button may bring nuclear devastation. And at the level of individual living there are increasing evidences of mental disorders, delinquency, and a rampant secularism. These forebode an uncertain tomorrow. Hence the repeated request, "Please tell me how to face the future."

One affirmation which cheers the believer is this: "Jesus Christ the

same yesterday, and to-day, and for ever" (Heb. 13:8). At the beginning of this century Maltbie D. Babcock wrote a hymn which has
not lost its central truth:

> This is my Father's world,
> O! let me ne'er forget
> That though the wrong seems oft so strong,
> God is the ruler yet.

God has not resigned; nor has he been pushed aside; nor has he
accepted an emeritus status. Nineteen hundred years ago there were
men who thought that hope was lost, but Easter followed Good Fri-
day. This is the divine sequence! "And I heard as it were the voice
of a great multitude, and as the voice of many waters, and as the
voice of mighty thunderings, saying, Alleluia: for the Lord God
omnipotent reigneth" (Rev. 19:6).

Another affirmation which cheers the believer is that we are required to live only one day at a time. To a people who were also full
of misgivings and fears concerning the unknown future, Jesus said,
"So do not be anxious about tomorrow; tomorrow will look after
itself. Each day has troubles enough of its own" (Matt. 6:34, NEB).
We shall be too burdened to rise if we attempt to carry yesterday's
guilts and tomorrow's apprehensions as well as today's responsibilities.

A third affirmation which cheers the believer is that we neither live
today nor face tomorrow alone. We walk with the living Christ who
unfolds to us his truth and his vision, even as he did to the two
disciples on the road to Emmaus. And he conveys to us his joy of
life, his love for man, his dreams for us, and his work in which we
must accept a share.

One day Douglas Southall Freeman, engrossed in thoughts about
the problems of the world, almost stumbled over a little child. The
youngster looked up into his face and said, "Dr. Freeman, you just
about stepped on me." The great journalist and Pulitzer Prize bi-
ographer told me later, "I realized then and there that the real challenge of life is so to live and serve as to keep that smile and that light
in the face of that little child and others like her."

Even as we may clasp the hand of a child and give him confidence
to take the next step, so our companion Christ offers his hand and
bids us walk faithfully in his way toward the gateway leading beyond
today to a brighter and better tomorrow.

2.

How to Face Up to Life

I SHALL NEVER FORGET the thrill I experienced as a young man when I visited Yosemite Park in California and spent a night in the valley between towering walls of granite. After darkness had come in the valley I was told that I should not miss seeing the firefall. No one had told me about this, and I had not the slightest idea what firefall meant. Then after all lights in the valley had been extinguished or dimmed, a voice called out, "Let the fire fall!" A river of burning embers cascaded down the rugged side of a cliff. It was a beautiful and memorable sight.

Later I was told that great fires were built at the top of the cliff, and at the appropriate moment the hot coals were pushed from that great height to the valley floor a mile or so below.

In the Old Testament is found the story of an even more remarkable firefall atop Mount Carmel. This story centers in the prophet Elijah. From what happened to him we can learn some lessons about facing up to life, for that is what Elijah had to do.

This ninth-century prophet lived in a difficult and desperate time. Life was perilous for a man of God. First, he was threatened continually by Jezebel, a woman whose name, perhaps more than that

11

of any other woman in history, is the incarnation of evil. A Phoeni-
cian princess, she married Ahab, the king of Israel, and came into
Canaan determined to destroy the religious faith of Abraham's off-
spring and in its place established Baalism, a licentious and vulgar
cult that at every point was at variance to the worship of God. She
brought four hundred and fifty priests of Baal to assist her. The Bible
records in candid detail the chronicle of her evil endeavor. Edith
Deen has written:

> In her evil power over her husband, Jezebel might be compared to
> Shakespeare's Lady Macbeth. In her fanaticism, she might be likened to
> Mary, Queen of Scots. Her death, though far more bitter and bloody, sug-
> gests the death on the guillotine of another alien queen, Marie Antoinette.
> And like Catherine de Medici, Jezebel is remembered as an outstanding
> example of what a woman ought not to be.[1]

And the full force of her evil genius was hurled at Elijah.

Secondly, Elijah was the object of Ahab's scheming. Militarily
valiant and morally weak, he fell in with his wife's malignant machina-
tions and permitted idolatrous worship within the shadow of the
palace. His wicked intent is vividly illustrated in his destruction of
Naboth, a farmer who would not sell his father's vineyard to the
acquisitive king. The biblical historian telescopes the life story of
Ahab into a single verse: "And Ahab did more to provoke the Lord
God of Israel to anger than all the kings of Israel that were before
him" (1 Kings 16:33). And that's saying something! Imagine the
role of a man of God in a kingdom over which such people as Ahab
and Jezebel reign!

Thirdly, Elijah was commanded by God to confront Ahab and to
speak boldly and unequivocally to this king who respected neither
God nor man. A famine fell upon Israel. So great was the devastation
wrought by the drought that the king himself searched throughout the
land for water to save his horses. It was Elijah's unhappy responsibility to inform the king that the rains had ceased because of the
idolatry of king and people and that no healing rains would come
until they desisted from their evil practices. Rains would come as a
divine blessing only upon a deserving people. But Ahab, blaming
Elijah and rejecting any personal responsibility, hurled at the prophet
the epithet "you troubler of Israel" (1 Kings 18:17, RSV).

When the situation became critical, Elijah knew that the psycho-
logical moment had come. He proposed that a contest should be held

to determine the sovereignty of God or Baal. Subsequently the people assembled on Mount Carmel where occurred one of the most dramatic scenes in biblical literature and indeed in all literary annals. After the priests of Baal and Elijah had each built altars, the prophet said, "Call ye on the name of your gods, and I will call on the name of the Lord: and the God that answereth by fire, let him be God. And all the people answered and said, It is well spoken" (1 Kings 18:24).

First of all, the priests of Baal called upon their god and they continued their petitioning throughout the day. After a time, Elijah needled them, saying, "Shout . . . for he is a god! He is musing, or away on business, or perhaps he is asleep and must be wakened!" (1 Kings 18:27, MOFFATT).

After their pleas failed, Elijah asked that twelve barrels of water be poured on God's altar and then said in substance, "Let the fire fall! Let the fire fall!" And a consuming flame from heaven burned the sacrifice, the wood, and the altar stones. In awe the people fell on their knees and cried, "The Lord, he is the God; the Lord, he is the God" (1 Kings 18:39).

After Elijah had ordered the execution of the priests of Baal, there remained the matter of the rain. The prophet prayed, stopping on seven occasions only long enough to dispatch his servant to the mountaintop to ascertain the signs in the skies. The seventh time the servant reported seeing "a little cloud out of the sea, like a man's hand" (1 Kings 18:44). Soon the rain came in torrents.

After the rain there remained the wrath of Jezebel. Her loss of the priests had incensed her, and she sent a message to the prophet: "So let the gods do to me, and more also, if I make not thy life as the life of one of them by to-morrow about this time" (1 Kings 19:2). Knowing that her threat represented more than idle words, Elijah fled a day's journey into the wilderness where, sitting under a juniper tree, he indulged himself in self-pity, bemoaned his fate, and longed for death. But the Lord aroused him, and the prophet traveled for forty days and forty nights until he reached the holy mountain where, generations earlier, the Lord had bestowed on Moses the tablets of the law. There after the passing of wind, storm, and fire, the Lord spoke to him in a still small voice. And God said, "What doest thou here, Elijah?" (1 Kings 19:13). The prophet lamented the times and seasons, but God told him that he must undertake more mighty works. So Elijah arose and went back to face up to life again.

This is a wonderfully moving story, and in its pages may be found lessons that will help us to do for ourselves what Elijah learned to do in facing up to life.

I

The first lesson is *to face life as it is,* not as we wish it were, nor as we think it ought to be, nor as we hope someday it will be, but as it is—good and bad, promising and depressing, hopeful and despairing, pleasant and harsh. We must beware of the temptation to escape through isolation or indulgence or self-pity. Escape will not ease our heartaches or solve our problems. I asked a man who had succumbed to alcohol, "Does a bottle help you to find answers for your problems?" "No, not really," he replied. "They're still there in the morning—and sometimes there are more problems than before."

We are helped in our facing up to life when we realize that God put us in this world and made us what we are. This is the kind of world and situation in which he wishes us to engage in heroic Christian struggle and endeavor. I was thinking along these lines one day when I attended worship in an old church in the Northern Neck of Virginia. A young preacher, whom I had not previously met, quoted in the course of his sermon a sentence which he attributed to an eighteenth-century source:

If you would know the short and simple way to the happiness of the Christian life, learn to thank God and praise Him for everything that happens to you.

At that time I was recuperating after a heart attack, and these words were a spiritual tonic to which I was immediately responsive. Each of us would do well to take to heart the resolution of the Apostle Paul, "I have learned, in whatsoever state I am, therewith to be content" (Phil. 4:11). Often we have no alternative other than to face life as it is. Elijah had no other choice.

II

The second lesson we learn from Elijah's experience—and it is no less important than the first one—is *to resist the tendency to blame*

God for the evil, sorrow, and sadness that darken our lives. We must shoulder these troubles and seek whatever lesson or blessing they have to offer. Surely we are wrong to blame God for the evil other men do or that we have brought upon ourselves.

When one calamity after another had catapulted Job to the lowest depths of misery, his wife told him to "curse God, and die" (Job 2:9), and his three so-called comforters counseled capitulation and resignation, but Job cried unto the Lord, "I know that thou canst do every thing, and that no thought can be withholden from thee. . . . Therefore have I uttered that I understood not; things too wonderful for me, which I knew not. . . . Wherefore I abhor myself, and repent in dust and ashes" (Job 42:2-3, 6).

When the drought plagued Israel, God provided a sanctuary for Elijah where he might drink from the brook Cherith and to which ravens came with food in the morning and evening. "And it came to pass after a while, that the brook dried up, because there had been no rain in the land" (1 Kings 17:7). This was a crucial point in the testing of Elijah's faith. He might well have felt justified in saying, "So this is the kind of God I have trusted in! Now he makes dry the stream of water upon which my very life depends." But Elijah did not hurl defiance at the Lord. He knew that in our world God "maketh his sun to rise on the evil and on the good, and sendeth rain on the just and on the unjust" (Matt. 5:45). Elijah would not censure God for the drought which he believed a wicked people had brought as a judgment upon themselves. In a world that has been corrupted by the unrighteous, even the righteous feel pain. Yes, and even God "spared not his own Son" (Rom. 8:32).

III

A third lesson which we may glean from the story of Elijah is that it is important *to share life with other people*. After his experience at the Brook Cherith, Elijah was sent by the Lord to Zarephath, for "behold, I have commanded a widow woman there to sustain thee" (1 Kings 17:9).

The widow had zealously guarded the little bread she had left against the day when she and her son might face a final need for nourishment. This the prophet requested for himself, seemingly with the thought that his need was greater than their need and that he had better get while the getting was good. But not so. Rather Elijah was testing the widow's trust in the providence of God. And the morsel, which the woman generously surrendered, was miraculously multiplied according to their requirement. Because Elijah shared his faith with others and because the widow shared what she had, each benefited.

Paul wrote, "Bear ye one another's burdens, and so fulfil the law of Christ" (Gal. 6:2). We are meant to share the needs, sorrows, and problems of our human brethren. A genuine empathy is one of the noblest of Christian virtues. Alone in his retreat by the Brook Cherith Elijah was no more than half a man. By identifying his lot with the widow and her son, he partook of the joys and sorrows of fellowship and was the better for it.

Is this not a ministry which is incumbent upon us as Christians in a generation when so many people hunger, are spiritually displaced, and long for a warm-blooded response to their loneliness? It is not enough that we place our offerings, however generous, upon the collection plates in church or that we offer prayers, however earnest, in behalf of a troubled humanity. We must embrace mankind in love, heart to heart and hand to hand, even as Elijah clung to the widow's son in his mortal sickness and so *loved* him back to health.

Emerson abbreviates a great truth into a simple thought:

Rings and jewels are not gifts, but apologies for gifts. The only gift is a portion of thyself. Therefore the poet brings his poem; the shepherd, his lamb; the farmer, corn; the miner, a gem; the sailor, coral and shells; the painter, his picture; the girl, a handkerchief of her own sewing.[2]

The central message of this lesson from Elijah's experience seems to me to have been well expressed in the following poem:

> I do not thank Thee, Lord,
> That I have bread to eat while others starve;
> Nor yet for work to do
> While empty hands solicit Heaven;
> Nor for a body strong
> While other bodies flatten beds of pain.
> No, not for these do I give thanks!
>
> But I am grateful, Lord,
> Because my meagre loaf I may divide:

> For that my busy hands
> May move to meet another's need;
> Because my doubled strength
> I may expend to steady one who faints.
> Yes, for all these do I give thanks!
>
> For heart to share, desire to bear,
> And will to lift,
> Flamed into one by deathless Love—
> Thanks be to God for this!
> Unspeakable! His Gift!³

A lovely lady was called upon to face alone a terrible tragedy that might well have turned her from God and caused all that was good within her to die. But by the grace of God she has come through her ordeal, not bitter, but better in spirit and radiant in personality. So great has been the blessing her life bestows on others that scores of people thank God for the faith, life, and witness she shares so generously.

"How have you done it?" I asked her.

"Let me show you," she said, and she wrote down for me a verse which has inspired her. It is this:

> How can we hope to be mowers,
>   And to gather the ripe gold ears,
> Unless we have first been sowers
>   And watered the furrows with tears?
>
> It is not just as we take it,
>   This mystical world of ours,
> Life's field will yield as we make it
>   A harvest of thorns or of flowers.⁴

"That's what I live by," she said, adding, "And there's another sentiment which I cherish equally: 'If we would read the secret history of our enemies, we would find in each man's life sorrow and suffering enough to disarm all hostility.' "

God adds to the shared life that particular blessing which each of us needs, and he promises that the harvest of our lives will be flowers, not thorns.

IV

The fourth lesson which comes to us from the experiences of Elijah is *to face sin and evil with God-given courage,* trusting the Lord to do his part as we do ours. When Elijah challenged the priests of Baal, he was completely confident that, having done his best, his Lord would come through. And God did—and he always will. In the case of Elijah, fire and rain came from heaven. I do not know how God will respond to your necessity, but I do know that when you have chosen to labor with God, all of the resources of the Eternal will be there to sustain you.

Elijah underscored the importance of making a choice when he called the people to Mount Carmel: "How long halt ye between two opinions? if the Lord be God, follow him: but if Baal, then follow him" (1 Kings 18:21). The figure of speech he uses describes a man who hops first on one leg and then on the other. That is what the children of Israel were doing in their vacillation between loyalty to God and to the sensuous, free-and-easy appeal of Baal. "How long will you hobble on this faith and that?" (MOFFATT). Elijah requires that they make a choice—if Baal, then you must accept the consequences; if God, then I'll show you what he will do.

As for Elijah, he had made his choice, and it required courage and a stout heart. But he knew there was a spiritual bank account that was as inexhaustible as the mercies of God. We too may draw from this resource according to our needs.

V

A final lesson which the narrative concerning Elijah teaches is *to refrain from surrendering to discouragement and frustration.* Having escaped from the wrath of Jezebel, Elijah "sat down under a juniper tree" (1 Kings 19:4) and indulged himself in the doubtful luxury of self-pity. He permitted his doubts to overcome his faith. Failing to realize that the hour of apparent tribulation may be in fact the hour of greatest triumph, he merely doubled his miseries.

Each of us has a favorite juniper tree whose shade we covet when we have exhausted our own strength and have forgotten or disbelieved that God has guaranteed to strengthen us. At such times we turn from life and argue that we have been victimized by cruel circumstance. And all the time there is, as there was for Elijah, a cake and a cruse of water within arm's reach and a ministering angel nearby. The answer for our juniper-tree despondency lies in the discovery that happiness and joy are to be found, not in what we can do for ourselves, but in what in God's name we can do for others. Always when we listen attentively and faithfully, we shall hear the still small voice of the Eternal.

> I heard the voice of Jesus say,
>   "Come unto Me and rest;
> Lay down, thou weary one, lay down
>   Thy head upon My breast."
>
> I came to Jesus as I was,
>   Weary, and worn, and sad;
> I found in Him a resting-place,
>   And He has made me glad.[5]

Discouragement thwarts our judgment and invariably leads us to the deception that our plight is far worse than that of other men. By encouraging our feelings of discouragement we tend to become egotistical, self-centered, and frustrated.

Listen to Elijah's lament: "I have been very jealous for the Lord God of hosts: because the children of Israel have forsaken thy covenant, thrown down thine altars, and slain thy prophets with the sword; and I, even I only, am left; and they seek my life, to take it away."

God broke into Elijah's undue self-concern, saying, "Yet I have left me seven thousand in Israel, all the knees which have not bowed unto Baal, and every mouth which hath not kissed him." (1 Kings 19:14, 18.)

God told his prophet to face up to life as it was, to refrain from blaming the Almighty, to share his life with the children of Israel and with Elisha who would need counsel and guidance, and courageously to continue that work to which he had been divinely called.

Elijah rose to the challenge. King Ahab died ignominiously in battle. Queen Jezebel was at last thrown to the ground where dogs devoured her mortal remains. But Elijah bequeathed to Elisha, his successor, a double portion of his spirit, died not after the fashion of men but was taken to heaven in a fiery chariot, and later reappeared with Moses on the Mount of Transfiguration.

Elijah had indeed mastered the lesson taught centuries later by our Lord, who "stedfastly set his face to go to Jerusalem" (Luke 9:51), and said to his disciples, "Behold, we go up to Jerusalem; and the Son of man shall be betrayed unto the chief priests and unto the scribes, and they shall condemn him to death" (Matt. 20:18). For those who really wish to face up to life, the eternal Christ shows the way.

On the front porch of a hotel Dr. Norman Vincent Peale engaged in a conversation with a young man who soon revealed that, because of an alcoholic, faithless father and a malcontent mother, he was determined never to marry. Sensing the utter misery of the youth, Dr. Peale tried to use psychology to get through to the real trouble, but he got nowhere.

Then he asked, "Has anybody ever told you about Jesus Christ?"

"I've heard the name," the young man replied.

"You mean in profanity?"

"Yes, that's about it."

Dr. Peale told him how Jesus came to meet the needs of men and women, to set an ideal for life, and to help people face up to life with confidence and power.

Finally the pastor persuaded the young man to pray. "Lord, I do need you," he said. "I can't help myself. Dr. Peale cannot do it for me. Will you help me?"

Months later Dr. Peale heard from the young man whose letter concluded with the words, "Why didn't anybody ever tell me about Jesus Christ before?"

We do not need to face life alone. When we say, "Lord Christ, I need you," he will be, as he promised, our divine companion and we too will be able to face up to life.

3.

How to Look at Yourself

AMONG SOME OLD SERMON notes of my father, who for many years served as a Baptist minister, is one page that particularly intrigues me. At the top of the sheet are these words: "Look at Ourselves." Whenever I read what he wrote, I look at myself, as it were, through his eyes. Here is a portion of the notes jotted down in his own handwriting:

Turn yourself inside out. Would you hire yourself? Would you wish to work for yourself?

If you found something not belonging to you and no one knew about it, would you look for the person who lost it?

We have need of patience with ourselves and with others. Wrong feeling is more infectious than wrong doing.

The fearful unbelief is unbelief in yourself.

If it is not decent, never do it; if it is not true, never speak it.

Live for something. Do good. Write your name in kindness, love, and mercy on the hearts of those you come in contact with, and you will never be forgotten. Your name will be as legible on the hearts you leave behind as are the stars on the brow of evening. Good deeds shine as the stars of heaven.

May I be no man's enemy. May I never quarrel with those nearest me; and if I do, may I be reconciled quickly. May I never devise evil against any man.

May I wish for all men's happiness and envy none. May I never rejoice in the ill fortune of one who has wronged me.

Is this not substantially the behavior which Paul prescribed for the Corinthians? "The Christ you have to deal with is not a weak person outside you, but a tremendous power inside you," he wrote, adding, "You should be looking at yourselves to make sure that you are really Christ's" (2 Cor. 13:3, 5, PHILLIPS).

Paul knew that the Corinthians needed this counsel. They resided in a notoriously wicked city, where the sins of the flesh were a continuing temptation. But Paul also discerned that they were guilty of sins of the spirit, for they condemned one another and in a rather supercilious fashion compared themselves, not unfavorably, with other Christians. Paul rightly admonished them, "You ought to know by this time that Christ is in you, unless you are not real Christians at all" (2 Cor. 13:5, PHILLIPS).

"To see oursels as ithers see us"[1]—and as God sees us—may become a profoundly revealing and disturbing experience. Do you remember the story of the little chimney sweep who one day while working stumbled into a beautiful white room? In a bed a golden-haired girl was asleep between immaculate sheets. In the midst of such spotlessness, the grime-covered lad saw himself in a mirror and realized how very dirty and black his face and hands were. He dashed from the room and in a nearby stream he scrubbed the soot from his hands and face. Then, looking at his reflection in the water, he actually saw his real self for the first time!

To look honestly at ourselves may bring a redeeming, transforming experience. I am not thinking of our outward appearance but more especially of that inner self which is known only to ourselves and to God. In life's crises other people may gain momentary insights of our inner being—the self that we must live with and put up with every single day.

A very self-satisfied man, who had done many evil things and had cherished wrong purposes in his heart, was nonetheless well thought of in the community. He even regarded himself quite highly. One night he dreamed that, smartly dressed in a long white robe, he was walking along the golden streets of heaven. "Well, I made it!" he commented with smug satisfaction. "I got away with all of that and no one is the wiser." Yet he felt uneasy and uncomfortable. Other people stared curiously at him. They seemed to be looking, not at him, but through him. Then, looking closely at himself, he discovered that his black heart showed from beneath his white robe. He awakened in a cold sweat and determined that some things within himself needed to be drastically changed.

Not only after a troublesome dream or when confronted by some dire circumstance, but in a day-by-day spiritual inventory, we need to examine ourselves closely. Such searching questions as these will do as starters:

Am I really Christian in all of my dealings and associations with others?

Are my motives, ambitions, and actions truly Christlike?

During the years have I forgotten some high ideals and neglected worthy goals?

Have I learned the stringent demands of a meaningful self-discipline?

Do I make allowances and offer excuses for myself regarding behavior I will not tolerate in others?

Am I so self-contented that I no longer aspire to higher things?

The Federal Reserve Bank of Dallas published a little chart which calls for a revealing self-evaluation:

COULD YOU PASS A TEST LIKE THIS?

If you were to be judged today and asked if you could honestly subscribe to the following formula—

That you have been just to those who need help, whether you like them or not,

That you have been sympathetic and tolerant,

That you have been understanding when inclined to criticism,

That you have been grateful for the small favors of life and have shared them with others,

That you have accepted your task in life as a privilege and have honored it,

That you have returned kindness for kindness and in some small way tried to make the world a better place to live in for yourself and for others—

Would you like to be able, without reservation, to write your name here?

. . . .

To pass such a test we shall need the encouragement which we may claim for ourselves from the promise, "The Christ you have to deal with is not a weak person outside you, but a tremendous power inside you." The difference this power makes is shown in a letter which an airline stewardess wrote to her pastor:

Our church has played a major role in every phase of my life. The inspiration of your sermons has made a deep impression for good in my personality. In myself and in the lives of my friends I see definite evidences of the miracles which your preaching and the grace of God have wrought. Warped personalities have been straightened, broken homes have been saved, and talented people have turned their abilities into productive channels. I think the real secret is that you help people to examine themselves, to live a first-hand religion, and to stand on the strength God offers, knowing they need no artificial crutches on any occasion.

II

When we look honestly at ourselves, it becomes obvious that we must choose between two ways of living. One is the way of self-seeking, self-pity, self-satisfaction, and self-esteem. Do you worship the man you see in a mirror? Do you feel that you are right and others are wrong? Are other people merely instruments and means to serve your ends?

The Christian, on the other hand, follows the way of Christ. He strives for self-respect through self-discipline, self-denial, self-giving, and self-discovery. The Apostle Peter learned of the vast difference between the way of the world and the way of incarnate love after he saw himself through the eyes of Jesus. Peter, a roughhewn and rugged man whose temperament was impetuous and fiery, was challenged by Jesus, "Thou art Peter, and upon this rock I will build my church; and the gates of hell shall not prevail against it" (Matt. 16:18). Such a challenge Peter could not turn from. The transformation of the apostle did not come overnight. We read that during those harried hours before our Lord's crucifixion Peter turned from the way of light. He denied his Lord, but when he came to himself, he wept bitterly and in genuine penitence. Once more he looked at life from Christ's point of view. Tradition crowns the story of Peter's courageous, humble, and self-giving life by telling us that when at last he was required to pay as a martyr his last full measure of devotion, Peter begged that he might be crucified with his head down, for he felt unworthy to die after the manner of his Master.

The Apostle Paul also knew the difference Christ brings into life. When he looked at himself, was he proud and arrogant? Read these words from his own hand: "O wretched man that I am! who shall deliver me from the body of this death?" (Rom. 7:24). Was there anywhere an answer to his lamentation? He found his answer in Christ's promise: "My grace is sufficient for thee: for my strength is made perfect in weakness" (2 Cor. 12:9).

How disheartening it can be to see ourselves as we really are, but how encouraging to see ourselves as God sees us and to know that we are children of a heavenly Father who both cares and can help us.

In Lloyd C. Douglas' moving narrative, *The Robe,* there is an episode emphasizing that "the Christ you have to deal with is not a weak person outside you, but a tremendous power inside you":

"Where do you think [Jesus] went?" asked Marcellus, huskily.

"I don't know, my friend. I only know that he is alive—and I am always expecting to see him. Sometimes I feel aware of him, as if he were close by." Justus smiled faintly, his eyes wet with tears. "It keeps you honest," he went on. "You have no temptation to cheat anyone, or lie to anyone, or hurt anyone—when, for all you know, Jesus is standing beside you."

"I'm afraid I should feel very uncomfortable," remarked Marcellus, "being perpetually watched by some invisible presence."

"Not if that presence helped you defend yourself against yourself, Marcellus. It is a great satisfaction to have someone standing by—to keep you at your best."[2]

Is there a more healing therapy than to look at ourselves as Jesus saw us—as sinners whom he could save, as unworthy children whom God had chosen to walk on higher roads, and as men who were worth his dying for? Paul had looked upon himself as an earnest and dedicated persecutor of Christians. In righteous wrath he pursued Christians with the same zeal which characterized his activity at every level of his life. He had watched approvingly when the martyr Stephen was stoned to death and when other Christians were imprisoned. Then on the Damascus road, the Master spoke directly to him: "Saul, Saul, why persecutest thou me?" (Acts 9:4). In that revealing moment when his eyes were blinded by a light not of this world, Paul saw himself as he really was and Christ as he really is. From that life-changing experience came Paul, the greatest missionary and outstanding witness of the Gospel. And from the insight and revelation of that hour came the conviction which he wrote to the Corinthians: "You should be looking at yourselves to make sure that you are really Christ's."

When we look at ourselves through the eyes of Christ, we can no longer remain diffident or casual. He calls us to make a choice and a decision. We find in John Oxenham's familiar words the sense of urgency which a confrontation with Christ brings to everyone:

> To every man there openeth
> A Way, and Ways, and a Way,
> And the High Soul climbs the High Way,
> And the Low Soul gropes the Low,
> And in between, on the misty flats,
> The rest drift to and fro.
> But to every man there openeth
> A High Way, and a Low,
> And every man decideth
> The Way his soul shall go.[3]

4.

How to Become More Than You Are

THE SUBJECT OF THIS chapter was suggested by Margueritte Harmon Bro's very helpful little book entitled *More Than We Are*. Her thesis is that each of us wants to be more than we are because potentially we are more than we really are at any given moment.

Throughout life we are more than we are and we also want to be more than we are. A small child dreams of being a fireman, policeman, pilot, or spaceman. As a teenager, he longs for the day when, as an adult, he may claim all of the rights and liberties of maturity and have a home and children of his own. In the midst of his career, he anticipates the privilege of giving his children the things he didn't have and hopes they will achieve all he aspired to but failed to realize. Then later his mind will build a bridge to Eternity where, freed from the limitations of the flesh, he knows he will be more than he is now.

This thrust beyond the actual to the potential is a God-given thought. The poet of ancient Israel expressed this idea: "As the hart panteth after the water brooks, so panteth my soul after thee, O God" (Ps. 42:1). Another has put it in these words:

> No vision and you perish;
> No ideal, and you're lost;

27

> Your heart must ever cherish
> Some faith at any cost.
>
> Some hope, some dream to cling to,
> Some rainbow in the sky,
> Some melody to sing to,
> Some service that is high.[1]

But to hitch your wagon to a star and to say that "old men shall
dream dreams" and "young men shall see visions" (Joel 2:28) represents more than vain and idle longings to reach beyond the fulfilled
to the unfulfilled. God has so structured our human nature that we
are divinely discontented with things-as-they-are. He has put the
upward reach into the heart of man.

John Steinbeck reads well our nature:

> The last clear definite function of man—muscles aching to grow, to
> work, to create beyond the single need—this is man. To build a wall, to
> build a house, a dam, and in the wall and house and dam to put something
> of Manself, and to Manself take back something of the wall, the house,
> the dam; to take hard muscles from the lifting, to take the clear lines and
> form from conceiving. For man, unlike any other thing organic or inor-
> ganic in the universe, grows beyond his work, walks up the stairs of his
> concepts, emerges ahead of his accomplishments.[2]

We turn to this subject in the knowledge, not only that man very
much wishes to be more than he is, but also that God desires and expects him to become more. How then can we become more than we
are now?

I

We begin where all Christian thought begins—with Jesus Christ.
The Apostle Paul, writing to persons like us who were seeking a
higher life, said, "Ye are complete in him" (Col. 2:10). This verse,
according to two recent translations, reads, "It is in him that you
reach your full life" (MOFFATT) and "Your own completeness is
only realized in him" (PHILLIPS). Christians believe that Christ helps
them to live fully—completely—in the light of what God has revealed in him to be finest and best.

Paul testified to this Christian conviction when he wrote, "I am
crucified with Christ: nevertheless I live; yet not I, but Christ liveth

in me: the life which I now live in the flesh I live by the faith of the Son of God, who loved me, and gave himself for me" (Gal. 2:20). He admonished the Colossians, "As ye have therefore received Christ Jesus the Lord, so walk ye in him: rooted and built up in him, and stablished in the faith" (Col. 2:6-7).

The living Christ—Christ living in you as the Master and Lord of your life—is the key to becoming more than you are. But a namby-pamby loyalty to Christ or a take-it-or-leave-it discipleship increases neither the vertical nor the horizontal dimensions of life. Far too many Christians are similar to a character in one of Romain Rolland's narratives:

> Jesus hardly occupied his thoughts at all. It was not that he did not love him: he loved him when he thought of him: but he never thought of him. Sometimes he reproached himself for it, was angry with himself, could not understand why he did not take more interest in him. . . . In truth, if Jesus appealed to him, Beethoven did not less.[3]

If you insist on shutting Christ out and depending on your own sufficiency, you will have one kind of life. If, however, you accept Christ as Savior, you will have a far richer, finer life.

A little girl discovered after she had gone to bed that she could see reflected in the dressing-table mirror the picture of Jesus hanging on the wall behind her. When she sat up, however, she could see herself in the mirror but not Jesus. With a keener insight than she perhaps realized, she said, "Mommy, when I see myself in the mirror, I don't see Jesus, but when I see Jesus in the mirror, I don't see myself."

To see Jesus in the life of an individual is to see a far better person than he could ever be by himself. We are potentially more than we are now and more than we are alone.

II

We shall become more than we are when we truly realize that we have been made in God's image. God intends that we shall become more Christlike with each passing year. Our task in life is to discover how we may realize what a friend of mine calls our "possible best."

For example, here is a boy who plays a mediocre game of basket-ball. He has never quite measured up to what the coach expects of

him, and then in a particular game he begins to click. As he scores
one basket after another, the people say, "Well, that boy really has
arrived. Now he is living up to all of the advance billings. We knew
he had it in him. We've been waiting for it to come out."

Or here is a young man who has had an ordinary career. But suddenly in a crisis he measures up. The crisis draws out his hidden resources. What do we say concerning him? "He has found himself."
He has become the person God meant him to be.

The prodigal journeyed to a far country where he wasted his substance. Then the truth came to him that he was meant to be more
than a keeper of pigs in another person's sty. Jesus said of him, "He
came to himself" (Luke 15:17). "I can be more than this," the boy
must surely have said to himself. "This is not at all what my father
means me to be."

God made us in his own image and created us according to a plan
and purpose. If Christianity teaches any one thing, it is that we are
of value to him. Christ died for us, and his life was too precious to
be invested foolishly. Is it not for this reason that Paul said, "The life
which I now live in the flesh I live by the faith of the Son of God,
who loved me, and gave himself for me"?

That Christ gave himself for men is a distinctive Christian theme.
Some modern philosophies would deny that persons like us are that
valuable. The Communist philosophy asserts the supremacy of the
party and the state. The value of an individual is judged according to
his service to the party or the state. I was in the Ukraine some twenty-
five years ago shortly after officials had permitted thousands of human
beings to starve to death. Why would anyone be indifferent to such
human misery? The explanation is simply that these men and women
could not abide by the party's philosophy and refused to obey the
party's dictates. Therefore, they served no useful function. Similarly,
the Nazi philosophy separated the so-called sheep from the goats. On
the one hand were the blue-eyed and fair-skinned Nordics—"some-
bodies." On the other hand were the children of Abraham—"no-
bodies," who were permitted to starve and freeze or were gassed and
burned to death.

Christianity, rightly understood in terms of the mind and heart of
Christ, is no respecter of persons. Each person is of infinite value for
he is a child of God, fashioned in the divine image. God has a plan

and purpose for each of us. We are meant by virtue of our divine origin to be more than we are.

It is a memorable moment when we realize for a certainty that we are of value in God's sight. Because we are of primary worth to him, he should be given a primary place in our lives. It is this very realization of our individual worth that has aroused to action today so many of those who once were discriminated against and under-privileged.

III

We shall become more than we are when we rise to Christ's example and find our own avenues for serving mankind. We are to value our neighbor not because we admire his achievements nor because he speaks well of us or because he keeps a good house or for any other superficial reason. We are to love and serve men because they too are children of God. "God hath shewed me," said Peter, "that I should not call any man common or unclean" (Acts 10:28).

What must be our relationship to other men? Christ chose the role of a servant. Jesus "took upon him the form of a servant, and was made in the likeness of men" (Phil. 2:7). Can we reject the role he preferred? He said, "Whosoever will be chief among you, let him be your servant" (Matt. 20:27). Paul, following the example of his Lord, said, "I am a free man and own no master; but I have made myself every man's servant" (1 Cor. 9:19, NEB).

The truly great people in the world are doing the work of servants. Immediately the name of Dr. Albert Schweitzer comes to mind, but he only happens to be better known than hundreds of others who are also pouring out their lives in service to their fellow men and finding in return both joy and fulfillment.

Each of us has a part in this. Great as God is, he cannot do this work alone. He has a role for each of us. Without your desire, your will, and your decision, his work will not be complete. So within his Kingdom there is an indispensable place for you. Make your decision to find and fulfill it and help others to do the same.

In a letter from a dedicated Christian leader is this testimony to what an ordinary person—made truly extraordinary in terms of his acceptance of Christ's purpose—may do:

A good many years ago I had just moved to Richmond, Virginia, and I
went into a little store to buy a pair of socks. The clerk said, "You are
new here. Where are going to Sunday School and church?" I said, "Well,
I am not going anywhere." The clerk said, "Why don't you come next
Sunday to my Sunday School and go to church with me?"

The man wrote that this simple invitation changed his whole life,
for it opened the door to Christ as Lord and the fullness of life as
God meant it to be for him.

Each man has a part to play in the fellowship of those who are
trying to be more than they are and who know that God depends
upon them to help others discover the more abundant life.

IV

But you may ask, "How can I do this?" The answer is to be found
in the words Paul wrote. He had learned from Jesus how a man may
rise to God's requirement. He knew how Jesus had changed Peter
into an outstanding servant. He knew the transformation Jesus had
brought into the lives of John and others. Pre-eminently he knew
how on the Damascus Road Jesus had become for him a living
reality moving him to become more than he was. Paul learned, of
course, the price he must pay—"I am crucified with Christ"—and he
willingly paid it.

An earnest woman in India went on a long pilgrimage to find the
answer to her soul's desire, and finally after years of seeking found it
in Jesus Christ. Then her friends asked, "Now you will settle down,
won't you?" She replied, "I cannot settle down, for now I must go
on another pilgrimage, not as one who is seeking but as one who has
found." She had something to share, and she knew that in the shar-
ing she would find her greatest joy.

Paul has a second word for your consideration: "As ye have therefore received Christ Jesus the Lord, so walk ye in him: rooted and
built up in him, and stablished in the faith." We need to grow, and
this is a daily and lifelong process.

Is not the trouble with most of us that our roots do not go down
deep enough in Christ? Therefore, we do not bear the kind of fruit
he expects of us. In our generation of flux and crisis we should know

what we believe and why we believe it. Shallow soil will not sustain a lasting and vital Christian witness. This is possible only when we are established in our faith—rooted, grounded, and growing.

Too many grown persons try to make-do with a child's faith. Having said this, I can readily imagine that some reader chuckles to himself, thinking, "Preacher, I've got you there. Doesn't the Bible say that only as you become as a little child can you enter into the Kingdom?" True enough. But what is the most obvious characteristic of little children? They grow, are eager to learn, and always want to know more. Like them, we must grow in wisdom as well as in stature.

Paul wrote, "We are not meant to remain as children at the mercy of every chance wind of teaching and the jockeying of men who are expert in the crafty presentation of lies. But we are meant to hold firmly to the truth in love, and to grow up in every way into Christ, the head" (Eph. 4:14-15, PHILLIPS). He admonished his converts to be "rooted and built up in him, and stablished in the faith." Like a good schoolmaster—and millions to this day sit at his feet—Paul knew that growth is essential if we are to be more tomorrow than we are today.

When I visited in a delightful Virginia community, I was surprised to see a beautiful library, a handsome school, a lovely church, and other things not ordinarily found in a community of its size. I asked some townspeople, "How does this community happen to have so many attractive buildings?" They told me about a boy who had grown up there and attended a local church. Then he began to associate with the wrong people, committed a crime, and was sent to the penitentiary.

But the people in that church had faith in the young man and they loved him. They petitioned the governor, who acceded to their wishes and pardoned him. When he returned home, he was welcomed by those who respected the best in him. He determined to be that best.

In time he left that community and through determination and hard work acquired a fortune, but he never forgot the community that believed in him. He put stones over the graves of those who had forgiven and loved him. He cared for their loved ones as though they were his own. He built the library. He provided many civic improvements for the town that had helped him to become more than he was. The little church building was replaced, and over the door of the new one he inscribed these words:

THROUGH THE DIVINE LOVE THAT LIVES IN HUMAN HEARTS.

That divine love arouses our sleeping capabilities, stimulates our growth into the likeness of our Lord, motivates us to follow in the paths of service, and guides us as we strive to become more than we are and all God means us to be.

5.

How to Be Good and Good for Something

DRIVING HOME LATE ON a rainy night, a young minister suddenly was alerted to a fast train that was bearing down on him as he was approaching a railroad crossing. He knew he could not possibly stop in time on the wet-slick road. In a spilt-second decision he realized that his only hope for surviving was to cross the tracks ahead of the train. He made it—by inches. Immediately he pulled to the side of the road, for he was understandably shaken with fright and shock.

What thoughts fill a person's mind at such a time? In a letter to me he wrote, "As I became calmer, I kept asking, Why was my life spared? Why am I now living and not a statistic? What use does God wish to make of my life?" In that automobile at the roadside on that rainy night he dedicated himself anew to the service of his Lord.

Now in looking back across the years, I am convinced that his very useful life may in large measure be attributed to that crisis when he surrendered himself completely and unreservedly to God's most exacting purposes.

Few of us are called upon to face such an exigency, but each of us needs from time to time to ask himself these searching questions: How can I make my life count for something? How can I be good and do good? What am I good for?

Emphasis may be changed in the asking of the last question. What am I *good* for? That is, why be good? Or what am I good *for*? That is, am I good for something?

What are you good for? Certainly there is no justification in being good for evil reasons. Goodness is not goodness if it merely camouflages an arrogant pride. Goodness is only a veneer when it represents a pompous parading of artificially acquired virtues. Jesus said, "Take heed that ye do not your alms before men, to be seen of them" (Matt. 6:1). Nor should we be good only in response to pressures or for the sake of conformity, thereby making goodness a robe which covers an inner loathing. Such displays of goodness are "like unto whited sepulchres, which indeed appear beautiful outward, but are within full . . . of all uncleanness" (Matt. 23:27).

I

Why be good? *For the sake of one's own inner peace.* Guilt breeds fear and tension. We come to despise ourselves when we realize that we have settled for anything less than the best of which we are capable or that we have accepted anything lower than the highest we know.

> I have to live with myself, and so
> I want to be fit for myself to know,
> I want to be able, as days go by,
> Always to look myself straight in the eye;
> I don't want to stand, with the setting sun,
> And hate myself for the things I've done.[1]

Even as a little boy I learned that there is a mighty strong link between goodness and inner peace. Visiting one day in a neighbor's home, I saw two little souvenir coins which I took a fancy to and wanted for myself. When no one was looking, I put them in my pocket. But my joy in having them soon faded away. I showed them to a boyfriend, and he promptly asked the most natural question, "Where did you get them?" I knew I could not answer his question. I also knew I could never again share the coins with anyone. I found no peace until I threw them away. Then and there I determined never to take anything that belonged to another person. A gnawing sense of guilt costs too much in mental agony. The years since have taught me that peace of mind is a reward that comes in doing the best one knows.

Why be good? *For the sake of others who may suffer because of the wrongs one does and the sins one commits.* Time and again husbands or wives have wept as they told me of the domestic sorrows and tragedies caused by an unfaithful mate. Time and again parents have laid bare their hearts broken because of the sins of their chilren. Never shall I ever forget the anguish of a preacher-friend who came into my study and sobbed, "My son is a thief! My son is a thief!" Failure to do the right as God gives us understanding of the right deprives us individually of precious inner peace but also robs those who know and love us of the peace that our faithfulness should bring. Polonius discerned the relationship between oneself and others:

> To thine ownself be true
> And it must follow, as the night the day,
> Thou canst not then be false to any man.[2]

"It were better for him that a millstone were hanged about his neck," Jesus said, "and he be cast into the sea, than that he should offend one of these little ones" (Luke 17:2). The breadth of Christ's heart and teaching is such as to include not only "the little ones" but any man whom we may willfully cause to stumble or suffer.

Why be good? *For your own soul's sake.* Both biblical revelation and our daily experience validate the truth that "the wages of sin is death" (Rom. 6:23)—sometimes physical death and sometimes the death of that which is best in us. For the sinner sooner or later learns the high cost of low living.

An old story from the Yukon tells of two gold miners who spent a long winter together. With the return of spring they made plans to dispose of their findings, but each coveted all of the gold for himself. You can well imagine what follows. Each put poison in his partner's coffee. Then they realized what each had done to the other. As they lay dying, each knew that neither could claim the gold and both would die as murderers. The fearsome wages of sin! If for no more noble reason, you ought to be good for your own soul's sake.

Why be good? *Because goodness is the surest pathway to the enduring satisfactions of life.* We are often confronted with an inescapable choice between the difficult right or the easy wrong. Do you wish

lasting satisfactions or transient pleasures which pass with the morning dew? A wise man said, "Better is an handful with quietness [con-
tentment], than both the hands full with travail and vexation of
spirit" (Eccles. 4:6). Our Lord said to the Samaritan woman who
had sought the fleeting pleasures of sin and missed deep-flowing contentment, "Whosoever drinketh of the water that I shall give him
shall never thirst" (John 4:14).

An inexorable law of the spirit stipulates, "Cast thy bread upon
the waters: for thou shalt find it after many days" (Eccles. 11:1).
After World War II our government asked Dr. Herbert Gezork to
go to Germany to assist in the interrogation of former Nazis. One day
he sat at a desk opposite a young Nazi with whom he had grown up
in his hometown. They recognized each other and spoke of their
mutual friends and acquaintances. The one had chosen the Christian
way and had been forced to flee from Germany. The other had chosen
Hitler as his leader and now his life was in jeopardy. As the guard
led the German youth back to his prison cell, Dr. Gezork thought,
"There but for the grace of God go I." The one had chosen the fresh
air of freedom. The other was finally made to pay the price of his
own and his leader's sin.

Why be good? *For the sake of principles, ideals, and movements
to which you give the best that is in you.* Each of us *really* lives when
we live for something meaningful beyond ourselves. Such causes
challenge us to contribute our finest abilities and skills. Latent talents
are stirred up which we had not previously even dared to presume
that we possessed. For such causes we gladly make any sacrifice that
is required. We link our lives to the lives and aspirations of others
and God uses us all to his glory.

In a recent novel a character asks a question which each of us no
doubt has asked many times:

"Nan, how can I be happy? How *can* I?"

And Nan replies:

"It isn't for us to dictate, Harriet. . . . If you are happy, you are. You
can't make yourself unhappy. We are something, part of something, larger
than ourselves, Harriet."[3]

That which is "larger than ourselves" is ample reason for being good.
Shortly after World War II in London I saw a play that presupposed

that the Germans had conquered England and the English are struggling desperately to free themselves from the invaders. The young
heroine, who serves as a messenger between the leaders of the under-
ground freedom movement, is seized and tortured in the hope that
she will reveal the names of the leaders. At last she is sent back home
where, bruised, bleeding, and dying, she looks into her mother's face
and says, "Mother, I didn't say a word. I didn't say a word." Keeping
that secret cost her her life, but the cause for which she died triumphed
and the play closed with England free again.

Why be good? For the good of others and for a cause greater than
ourselves.

II

But it is not enough just to be good. We need to be good for something. The more important question is, What are you good *for*? The
rich young ruler told Jesus how good he was—"All these things have
I kept from my youth up" (Matt. 19:20). But when Jesus said,
"Come . . . follow me," he demurred. He was not good enough. By
way of contrast, note the measure of Christ's goodness: "Though
he was rich, yet for your sakes he became poor, that ye through his
poverty might be rich" (2 Cor. 8:9): Doctor F. W. Boatwright of
the University of Richmond took as the motto of his life the words of
William James, "The best use a man can make of his life is to spend
it for something that will outlast it."

We need to be good for the sake of the church and the Kingdom
of God.

> God sends no churches from the skies;
> Out of our hearts they must arise.[4]

If the church is to grow, prosper, and be strong in this generation of
peril and promise, then those who love her will need to give her their
last full ounce of devotion. What mark can you or I make in the on-
going movement of the church? Individually, we can do little, but
collectively the more than nine hundred million Christians in the
world can turn "the world upside down" (Acts 17:6), or as someone has said, "right side up." Have you stood up to be counted?

> You say the little efforts that I make
> will do no good; they never will prevail
> to tip the hovering scale
> where Justice hangs in balance.
>   I don't think
> I ever thought they would.
> But I am prejudiced beyond debate
> in favor of my right to choose which side
> shall feel the stubborn ounces of my weight.[5]

Shortly after World War I, St. Paul's Cathedral was judged to be resting upon insecure foundations. This hazard was promptly remedied. It is good that the foundations were strengthened, for within less than a generation bombs fell on London. Although the cathedral was hit, the building remained intact. Rising above the flames that engulfed the city was the cross of St. Paul's, which became for many a symbol of faith and hope. The church stood fast because of the sacrifice and devotion of those who in love had made her strong. Only as we give our strength, not to our church buildings only but also to the Living Church, the fellowship of believers in Christ, will His church accomplish her divine mission in this time of tension.

We need, furthermore, to be good for the sake of the tremendous issues of our day—racial justice, religious freedom, social righteousness, moral integrity, and peace among the nations—which solicit the energies of all men of good will. Progress in human relations does not just happen. Progress is made possible because of the dedicated and sacrificial exertions of committed Christians.

In their pursuit of radium Marie and Pierre Curie faced many heartbreaks and many failures. On one occasion Marie wrote:

> Life is not easy for any of us. But what of that? We must have perseverance and above all confidence in ourselves. We must believe that we are gifted for something, and that this thing, at whatever cost, must be attained.[6]

They returned again and again to their laboratory. Finally, their efforts bore fruit, all because this devoted couple were both gifted and good for something. A similar achievement crowns the efforts of all who determine to give their lives to the Kingdom of God. The victory will not come in a day, but the resolution is inevitable. "Thanks be unto God, which always causeth us to triumph in Christ" (2 Cor. 2:14).

But how can we be good for something? For the Christian the answer is found in the words which the rich young ruler rejected: "Come . . . follow me." No man is good for nothing. His goodness emanates from a corresponding cause or substantial motivation. "Keep thy heart with all diligence; for out of it are the issues of life" (Prov. 4:23). Here is where those who advocate goodness-without-God walk upon paper-thin ice. Whence comes the goodness they profess, if not from God? Whence the stimulation and nourishment, if not from God? Goodness apart from God soon degenerates into a shallow and insipid do-goodism.

This is illustrated in a lively mother-daughter conversation in one of the novels of John Galsworthy. Dinny is the first to speak:

"Providence is a wash-out, Mother. It's too remote. I suppose there is an eternal Plan—but we're like gnats for all the care it has for us as individuals."

"Don't encourage such feelings, Dinny; they affect one's character."

"I don't see the connection between beliefs and character. I'm not going to behave any worse because I cease to believe in Providence or an after life. . . . No; I'm going to behave *better*; if I'm decent it's because decency's the decent thing; and not because I'm going to get anything by it."

"But why is decency the decent thing, Dinny, if there's no God?"[7]

Yes. indeed, why?

A simple and lovely thing was said about Jesus: he "went about doing good" (Act 10:38). We are good for something when we imitate, according to our capacities and capabilities, His goodness. The thrust of His injunction, "Be ye therefore perfect, even as your Father which is in heaven is perfect" (Matt. 5:48), is yet to be completely felt in our lives, homes, and communities. But how wonderful will be the day when his followers take him at his word!

In a familar scene from the stage play, *Family Portrait*, Leban of Damascus speaks with Mary concerning her Son:

LEBAN: What did he teach?
MARY: Why—to—love your enemies—never to judge or condemn anyone —to be forgiving. And to make life as easy as you could for other people. To live for a purpose in which you believe and never let anyone keep you from your belief—not even your own family. You must be willing to die for it. And not to be afraid of people who kill the body. Because, after that, there is nothing more they can do. And to remember always that human life is beautiful—and noble—because it houses God.

I mean—when you degrade or dishonour human life—you degrade and dishonour God. That was all he taught.

LEBAN: Has anyone tried it—to live the way he taught?

MARY: I don't think so.

LEBAN: Might be interesting to see what would happen if they did.[8]

Which is to say, if they were to be good *for* something. By following Him we shall find forgiveness, guidance, strength, increasing joy and manifold opportunities for worthy service.

Edward Bok in his remarkable autobiography says that the secret of his life came from his great-grandparents who were sent by their king to serve on a barren island. They transformed it through the years into a place of beauty and a bird sanctuary to which scores of people came as visitors. To their descendants this noble couple bequeathed this priceless lesson: "Let the world be a little better and a little more beautiful because you have lived in it."

We too can go about both being and doing good—and being good for something.

6.

How to Be Like a Tree

WHENEVER I HEAR THE familiar words, "He shall be like a tree" (Ps. 1:3), my mind recalls the beautiful spruces which I admired while traveling in Norway. Those great pyramids of green foliage, rising often to a towering height and ever pointing toward heaven, are stanch and straight even though their roots must cling tenaciously to the meager soil on the rocky slopes.

Later when I spoke of those Norway spruces to a Christian friend who lives east of the Iron Curtain, he commented, "We Christians in my country are like those trees. Christian living for us is as difficult as survival must be for trees on barren mountainsides." Then he added this testimony: "But we are upheld by the grace and strength of God, and he enables us to point other men toward heaven."

Trees have long provided especially apt and congenial figures of speech by which to describe the Christian life. Joyce Kilmer found this to be true. When he was a student at Rutgers University, he became enamored by a three-hundred-year-old oak on the campus. Although showing the ravages of age, the tree, he knew, would live on, for each year new life sprang from the acorns that had fallen nearby. Inspired by that mighty oak, Kilmer wrote words which have enshrined both the tree and the poet in our memories:

43

> Poems are made by fools like me,
> But only God can make a tree.[1]

We, too, sense the wonder and inspiration of trees when we gaze
upon the ancient redwoods of California or stand beneath one of the
historic Constitution Oaks in the State of Virginia. Fifty of these oaks
still survive. Each has grown from a seedling given to one of the men
who met in a constitutional convention early in the century. The trees
are reminders of the work which the men labored together to complete.

Do you wonder that the Psalmist, when seeking to picture the godly
and righteous man, wrote, "He shall be like a tree"? This first psalm,
which introduces all of the poems in the Psalter, points to the contrast
between godly and ungodly persons. The righteous are stable, gracious,
prosperous, and fruitful; the unrighteous are unfruitful, vain, and
transient. A similar theme recurs throughout the Psalms. We are reminded in the Shepherd Psalm that God provides for the righteous
man: "The Lord is my shepherd; I shall not want. He maketh me to
lie down in green pastures: he leadeth me beside the still waters. He
restoreth my soul" (Ps. 23:1-3). In Psalm 121 we read: "I will lift
up mine eyes unto the hills, from whence cometh my help" (v. 1).
Elsewhere the poet declares, "God is our refuge and strength, a very
present help in trouble" (Ps. 46:1). And Psalm 103 assures us that
"like as a father pitieth his children, so the Lord pitieth them that fear
him" (v. 13).

I

The first Psalm tells us that the righteous man does not walk in the
counsel of the godless, nor stand in the way of sinners, nor sit in the
seat of the scornful. "Happy the man who never goes by the advice
of the ungodly, who never takes the sinners' road, nor joins the company of scoffers" (v. 1, MOFFATT). Many things are ruled out of his
life. He divorces himself from all that is evil. None doubts where he
stands in regard to both the ordinary contacts and the great issues of
life. He is "in the world but not of it." Though living in an evil generation, he turns from that which is unworthy of a man who has
committed his life to the Lord. With Martin Luther he resolves the predicament of choice by affirming, "It is neither safe nor prudent to do

aught against conscience. Here I stand—I cannot do otherwise. God help me. Amen."[2]

But our Christian life is a watered-down discipline if we merely abstain from evil. We need also the thrust of positive commitment. Of the godly man the Psalmist writes, "His delight is in the law of the Lord; and in his law doth he meditate day and night" (1:2). The divine word is the fountainhead of his belief and action. He has discovered the radiant truth that "in quietness and in confidence shall be your strength" (Isa. 30:15).

One evening when I was visiting in a Communist country, I was invited to the home of a godly Christian couple. Sitting at their little table, we ate plain and simple food—and shared an unforgettable fellowship. The good man of the house related some of the trials they had faced as they bore a faithful witness. The struggling Baptist church in their little village still proclaimed the divine word largely because of their sacrifice and devotion. Incredulously I asked, "How in the world do you withstand such persecutions and maintain your witness?" His response was a humble yet breathtakingly eloquent gesture. He lifted high his hand toward heaven. Truly his help came "from the Lord, which made heaven and earth" (Ps. 121:2). From beyond himself came that sure and steadfast undergirding which gave strength to his daily life and divine power to his sermons on Sunday.

II

What does it mean to be "like a tree"? The believer has, first of all, abundant resources, for he is planted, as it were, by the rivers of living water. Most of us can recall having seen beautiful trees growing along a riverbank in land that was for the most part barren of vegetation. Even as both marsh grass and great trees send their roots deep into the watery sod, so the Christian lays "a-hold on the greatness of God."[3]

A tree also continues to grow despite difficulties and disasters, and thereby not only fulfills its destiny but frequently becomes even stronger because of the besetting winds and storms. A tree on the campus of the University of Richmond has been an inspiration to many people, for when its top was broken in a storm it found strength to develop a sturdy new top. So greatly was the president inspired by that tree that when new branches replaced the old ones he erected a marker on which are inscribed these words:

LOOK AT ME AND TAKE HEART.

In a like manner the Christian, despite obstacles, grows and encourages others.

Thirdly, the Christian, like a tree, serves all men alike. The rain falls on the just and the unjust, and a tree offers shade to the good and the bad without drawing lines or making distinctions. Jesus said, "I am among you as he that serveth" (Luke 22:27). All who sought him were blessed by his healing touch and his words of wisdom. The inestimable joy of the Christian is to serve in his Master's name, remembering that "whosoever of you will be the chiefest, shall be servant of all" (Mark 10:44).

Furthermore, a tree shades others but cannot shade itself. Was it not written concerning Jesus, "He saved others; himself he cannot save" (Matt. 27:42)? Can the Christian do less or expect more? One of the finest missionaries I know served for a number of years in a hospital far out in the bush country in Africa. So isolated was the hospital that the government required that a landing strip be constructed so that in an emergency the missionary and his family might be evacuated by plane. Undaunted by distance and danger, my friend continued to serve with courage and conviction. Then one day a sick child coughed in his face and infection subsequently developed in one eye. He was flown home in an effort to save the sight of the eye and has returned to Africa with impaired vision but renewed dedication.

Finally, a tree not only offers shade but also generously provides rich fruit. This fruit varies according to the tree, even as human talents differ. Each of us is called to bear witness to the truth as we know it in Jesus Christ. It is from a context such as this that a fellow pastor offers these challenging words:

Many Christians have not advanced beyond the kindergarten stage in this tremendously important aspect of the Christian life, this business of self-giving. The discovery that our deepest happiness lies in serving depends wholly upon whether or not we serve. If service to others is an accomplished fact in our lives, if it is the climate in which we have our being, then the joy of service is for us self-authenticated and needs no argument or proof.

A friend once said to me, "I am prepared at any hour of the day or night to do any sort of thing that will help any mortal individual." Had I known nothing else about this person—his life has borne rich fruit—I would be certain that he is a true servant of God. His willingness to give himself does not root in the world's harsh way of grasping but is derived from a profoundly religious assumption regarding life. According to one of our Lord's most paradoxical teachings, "He that loseth his life for my sake shall find it" (Matt. 10:39). Truly to find genuine selfhood a man must surrender his own little interests in courageous devotion to a cause greater than himself. This in turn lifts him above himself.

If we attune our hearts to Christ, we shall hear him speaking:

Do you wish to be free? Then bind yourself.

Do you want to develop yourself? Then deny yourself.

Do you long for safety? Then meet danger head-on.

Do you crave security? Then share the problems of other men.

Do you seek contentment? Then bear another man's burden.

Do you desire happiness? Then join the fellowship of pain.

Do you covet power? Then shoulder responsibility.

Do you pray for peace? Then take up your cross and follow Him, for you will never find your life until you give it away.

Why did people cling to the hem of his garment? They knew he claimed nothing for himself and everything for them. The cardinal principle of his life and conduct was not "God for me," but rather "My life for others and for God." No man really lives until he lives for others.

III

Note further that the Psalmist says, "The ungodly are . . . like the chaff which the wind driveth away" (1:4). How graphic is the contrast he makes between the tree and the chaff! A tree stands strong and stable, pointing toward the heavens; but the chaff is tossed hither and yon by the wind and at last falls to the ground, far removed from the fruitful wheat.

Moreover, "the ungodly shall not stand in the judgment, nor sinners in the congregation of the righteous" (v. 5). One day "we shall all stand before the judgment seat of Christ" (Rom. 14:10). The New

Testament clearly pronounces the fateful words, "Depart from me" (Matt. 25:41). In that day those who have deluded themselves will understand the awesome truth, "Be not deceived; God is not mocked: for whatsoever a man soweth, that shall he also reap" (Gal. 6:7).

The words "I know you not" (Matt. 25:12), found in the parable of the wise and foolish virgins, recall an incident in Europe when I was guide for a group of American travelers. Fortunately, we were permitted to enter a famous museum after the regular closing hour. My responsibility as leader of the party was to identify those who were associated with me, for many others also tried to enter. As the people clustered about the door, I said either "Come in" or "I'm sorry." That day I understood a little more clearly the meaning of the words, "The Lord knoweth the way of the righteous: but the way of the ungodly shall perish" (Ps. 1:6).

We are confronted by the inescapable necessity of choosing between righteous and ungodly living, between life with Christ or death without him. As we make that choice, how good it is to hear the living Savior say, "I am the way, the truth, and the life: no man cometh unto the Father, but by me" (John 14:6). When we proclaim him as Savior, serve him as Lord, and share him with others, we know the full joy of life in his name. He will so strengthen us that we shall be like a tree planted by the rivers of water, and we shall bring forth good fruit in due season.

7.

How to Practice What You Preach

SOME READER WILL SURELY see the title of this chapter and then turn hurriedly to the next one, thinking that this one is meant particularly for preachers. But I mean that this chapter should speak to everyone—myself not least. The problem of matching words with actions and creeds with deeds is not limited to the pulpit or the pew, but embraces both.

You may recall Portia's familiar words:

If to do were as easy as to know what were good to do, chapels had been churches and poor men's cottages princes' palaces. It is a good divine that follows his own instructions. I can easier teach twenty what were good to be done than be one of the twenty to follow mine own teaching.[1]

The problem of practicing what one preaches involves every one of us. All men, when they think honestly, know that it is important to discover the things worth believing and to make every possible effort to see that our actions conform to the beliefs we profess.

A little boy looked closely at a group of older women who were sitting in beach chairs next to a swimming pool. Finally he approached one of the ladies and said, "Excuse me, Ma'm, but do you believe in God?" "Yes I do," she replied. "Do you go to church every Sunday?" he asked. "Yes," was her reply. "Do you read your Bible every day?"

"Yes," replied the somewhat surprised woman. "And do you say your prayers every night?" "Yes." "Good," he said, "then will you please hold my quarter while I go swimming?" He knew that there is an important relation between believing and behaving!

What we believe determines what we do, and our behavior reveals what we really believe. This is something Jesus stressed, and I am sure it was with some exasperation that he said, "Why call ye me, Lord, Lord, and do not the things which I say?" (Luke 6:46). These words come in Luke's counterpart of Matthew's Sermon on the Mount. Throughout the sermons in both gospels Jesus insists on the correlation between preaching and practicing. Here in Luke Jesus has just asked—I think with a touch of scorn—"Why do you look at the speck of sawdust in your brother's eye and fail to notice the plank in your own?" (Luke 6:41, PHILLIPS). Then he speaks of a good tree that bears good fruit, and adds, "Every tree is known by his own fruit" (Luke 6:44). He also compares two builders of houses. One lays the frame on rock, and the other on loose soil. "He that heareth, and doeth not, is like a man that without a foundation built an house upon the earth; against which the stream did beat vehemently, and immediately it fell; and the ruin of that house was great" (Luke 6:49). Jesus says that if we believe his words we must show our belief by what we are and what we do. As my friend Joseph Nordenhaug says with keen insight, "After all, your faith is what you believe plus yourself."

I

In this matter of practicing what you preach there are two important considerations. The first concerns what we believe. It is basically essential that we believe in Jesus Christ as Savior and Lord. If we do not as Christians believe this, then our faith is like a house of cards. "Believe on the Lord Jesus Christ, and thou shalt be saved" (Act 16:31). Just as positively the Bible says, "He that believeth not is condemned already, because he hath not believed in the name of the only begotten Son of God" (John 3:18). In his sermon at Pentecost Peter said, "Whosoever shall call on the name of the Lord shall be saved" (Acts 2:21). A belief such as this matters mightily, for it not only determines your eternal destiny but it also determines what you are, what you become, and what you do here and now.

We are to confess our faith in Christ and be baptized that the world may know where we stand. Our faith, of course, is individual and our commitment to Jesus is personal, but it is not private. It may be arrived at in secret, but we are not to keep it to ourselves. We could not keep it to ourselves if we wished to, for belief in Christ changes our lives and, sooner or later, others will see that our whole way of life has been altered. Not only is this change evident in the crises of life, but it shows in the routines of daily living.

After we have professed our belief in Christ as Lord and Savior, other beliefs naturally follow. We believe he has a purpose for our lives. We believe in his fellowship, the Church. We believe in the proclamation of his word to the uttermost ends of the earth. We believe that his Kingdom will come and his will shall be done on earth. All of these and more are beliefs that matter.

We shall need to study, think, and pray in order that our beliefs may grow and mature. In regard to our Christian convictions, there can be no status quo. If there is no growth, inevitably spiritual death follows.

One of the men who failed to climb Mount Everest was asked whether he thought anyone would ever succeed. "The doom of Everest is sealed," he said. "It will be climbed." When asked why he spoke with such certainty, he replied, "Because the limits of Mount Everest are fixed. It's just so high and no higher, but man grows in wisdom and in stature, and someday man will grow great enough to conquer the fixed mountain." And man did!

Another who did not reach the summit said, "Someday men will, but the men who do will be men of training and physical fitness and an unconquerable belief that it can be done."

II

Believing is very important, but it represents only one side of a coin. Who ever saw a one-sided coin? There must be a second side, and in this instance it is behaving. And that is just as important as believing.

Otherwise, why did Jesus say, "Why call ye me, Lord, Lord, and do not the things which I say?" and why did James write, "Be ye doers of the word, and not hearers only" (Jas. 1:22)? In the Sermon on the Mount Jesus made clear the divine basis of judgment: "Not every one

that saith unto me, Lord, Lord, shall enter into the kingdom of heaven;
but he that doeth the will of my Father which is in heaven" (Matt.
7:21). This is a test many fail to pass. John Hunter wrote a prayer
which we would do well to make our own:

> Dear Master, in Whose life I see
> All that I long and fail to be;
> Let Thy clear light for ever shine
> To shame and guide this life of mine.
>
> Though what I dream and what I do
> In my poor days are always two,
> Help me, oppressed by things undone,
> O Thou, Whose dreams and deeds were one.[2]

Believing and behaving, preaching and practicing, are each an imperative for Christians.

> Christian, rise, and act thy creed,
> Let thy prayer be in thy deed.[3]

The disciples John and Peter said, "We cannot but speak the things
which we have seen and heard" (Acts 4:20). And so must we. We
cannot believe that Jesus is Savior and Lord and believe that men are
lost apart from him, and not try to win others to this saving faith. We
cannot really believe that Jesus is "the way, the truth, and the life"
(John 14:6) and then say, "I don't care whether anyone else knows
this or not." The whole Christian mission to the world is predicated
upon the fact that we must proclaim our faith by word and deed. It is
our Lord's command and our joyous privilege and responsibility.

If we must "speak the things which we have seen and heard," then
there is no area of life in which the Christian faith is without relevance.
Consider, in the first place, the struggle for preference and position.
We preach humility and the desire to serve. Paul said, "In honour preferring one another" (Rom. 12:10) and "without preferring one before another, doing nothing by partiality" (1 Tim. 5:21). Yet even
within our churches all too often we place a premium on position and
commend the go-getter.

This striving for prominence is not a modern phenomenon. Jesus
felt called upon to rebuke the mother of two of his beloved disciples
when she asked that her sons be seated one on his right hand and the
other on his left in glory (Matt. 20:20-27).

In Robert Bolt's drama, *A Man for All Seasons,* Thomas More is finally brought to trial for his life. The key witness is an ambitious young man who has been told by the king that he will be given a place of honor in Wales if he will offer perjured testimony. So he stands before the court and speaks what everyone knows to be lies. Then More, who is condemned to die, looks directly at the young man and says, "What shall it profit a man to sell his own soul to gain the world, but you did it just for Wales." We sometimes sell ourselves so cheaply! And others look at us and say, "He preaches Christianity, but look how he behaves!"

Consider, secondly, how easily our faith is corrupted by the lure of mammon. It's an old, old story. Judas sold himself for thirty pieces of silver, and Ananias and Sapphira for a little gain betrayed themselves as well as the members of the struggling Christian fellowship in Jerusalem.

When I was a small boy my favorite baseball team was the White Sox, though that particular team later was called derisively the "Black Sox." During one fateful year the Sox had a wonderful line-up. The team went through a winning season and into the World Series, where they lost out. Afterward it was learned that some of the players had deliberately contributed to the loss by throwing games. A cartoon of the time pictured a group of youngsters outside of the locker room pleading with one of the players and saying, "Just tell us it ain't so." Some of us had to get new heroes.

When it comes to the desire for riches and the stewardship of money, do we practice what we preach?

Consider, thirdly, the problem of liquor about which there often seems to be a conspiracy of silence both within and without the church. Do we equivocate where we as Christians should stand firm? Does our practice as Christians parallel our commitment that our bodies are temples of the living God?

After reading an advertisement in a newspaper which portrayed Rudyard Kipling and Mark Twain indulging in a certain alcoholic beverage, a Midwestern clergyman wrote a letter to the editor. Mark Twain admittedly drank too much, and so did Kipling at one time. But, as the minister pointed out, Kipling came to the point where he wrote an article on why he gave up drinking. One night at a well-known drinking place he watched as two pimply young reprobates at a table nearby were intentionally persuading two girls to drink too much so that they might take advantage of them. Kipling recalled his disgust as the two young rascals led away the teenage girls. Their laughter echoed in his ear. Then and there he quit drinking, for he knew his seemingly innocent glass of beer was contributing to an institution that had degraded four young lives. Would we similarly seek to make our outward behavior conform to our inward commitment?

Consider, fourthly, our contemporary sexual standards. Looking upon today's illicit sex relations, unwed parents, immoral conduct on our motion picture and television screens, loose morals on our campuses, and unfaithfulness in our homes, would not Christ cry out, "Why call ye me, Lord, Lord, and do not the things which I say?"

I am sometimes almost amused when young people and those not so young think they have discovered something modern in sex. Nearly every possible expression of lascivious and lustful behavior is described in the Bible, and biblical heroes like David and Samson are not least among those who sinned in this regard. But the Book does not condone or apologize for such behavior, saying, for example, that after all we are weak-willed human creatures. Rather, the Book condemns all such immoral behavior. "The wages of sin is death" (Rom. 6:23), death to all that is good and worthy in us, death to wholesome human and family relationships, and death to our appreciation of ourselves and others as children of God. "Be not overcome of evil, but overcome evil with good" (Rom. 12:21). Here again do we as Christians live by the standards which we believe to be Christlike?

III

We can thank God that in our believing there is an answer to our sinfulness. This answer is Jesus Christ who brings the power of God to help us live according to our profession and to act according to our commitment. Robert Louis Stevenson, who knew the difference the coming of God made in his life, said, "My life came about like a well-handled ship, responding to the unknown steersman, God."[4]

Each of us has a stake here, for "all have sinned, and come short of the glory of God" (Rom. 3:23). But "if we confess our sins, he is faithful and just to forgive us our sins, and to cleanse us from all unrighteousness" (1 John 1:9). On our profession of that faith, we often sing:

> Happy day, happy day,
> When Jesus washed my sins away.[5]

It is a happy day, but that confession does not mark the end but the beginning of a new life.

Our spiritual journey is marked by hazardous detours. Our most stalwart resolution falters. Paul knew this to be true: "My own behavior baffles me. For I find myself not doing what I really want to do but doing what I really loathe" (Rom. 7:15, PHILLIPS). Then he exclaims, "It is an agonizing situation, and who on earth can set me free from the clutches of my own sinful nature?" Is there an answer? "I thank God there *is* a way out through Jesus Christ our Lord." (Rom. 7:24-25, PHILLIPS).

Would you take advantage of the love of our forgiving and redeeming Lord by saying, "I can sin as often as I want to because he will forgive me again and again"? Deep in our hearts we know that would be wrong and unworthy. "If a man love me," Jesus said, "he will keep my words" (John 14:23). God helping us, we shall live up to his expectations. This means that we will try to bring our preaching and our practice into a unified expression of our love for God.

A member of my parish told me about his brother, a beloved doctor. After a long and exemplary Christian life, he had a premonition that the end of his earthly pilgrimage was imminent. A week or so before his death, he called in his secretary and said, "I want you to bring the books up to date and write out a bill for everyone who owes me anything."

When this was done, the doctor looked at each one. "Now are all the books balanced?" he asked his secretary, and she said they were. Then he tore up every bill and threw the scraps in the wastebasket. "Now nobody owes me anything. It is all wiped clean."

If you had been indebted to that man, would you wish to take advantage of his good will or presume on his generosity? Would you not feel as I do when I see the Lord Christ dying on the cross and saying, "Father, forgive them"? I remember how often I have sinned and failed him and others, and said and done things I knew to be wrong. Looking to Christ Jesus, I am grateful that he was willing to pay the price for my sins and I covenant with him so to live as to be worthy of such love and sacrifice, so to live as to lead others to accept and serve him too.

8.

How to Know the Supreme Fact in Life

THE WORDS OF TWO laymen have combined to guide us at this point in our effort to meet head-on some of the more persistent questions that Christians ask. These laymen have never met and they do not know one another. But their individual suggestions have stimulated my thinking.

The first man had the responsibility of appraising the value of homes and property that must be destroyed to make way for the construction of a new road. After having surveyed carefully these properties—most of them residences belonging to relatively poor families—he said to me, "Something especially impressed me about these homes. In each one was some symbol or emblem or token of a religious faith—a Bible, a crucifix, or a religious picture. I was aware that each was a Christian home." Then he added, "Those people do not have much of this world's goods, but they have something far more important and far more worth while. They have the Christian faith."

We live in a day of rampant materialism, but many people are still conscious of that which is priceless and does not increase or diminish in value according to the fluctuations of the stock market.

The second layman asked me to read a short article he had written about Jesus Christ. About halfway through the article a particular sentence attracted my attention: "Jesus Christ is the supreme fact in life."

The second man had written something that was dramatically evident in the observations of the first. Each in his own way had spoken of the matchless sovereignty of Christ, whose supremacy is unrivaled in all human history. As one has well said, "Jesus' name is not so much written as ploughed into the history of the world." Millions of people join their voices in a single anthem of praise:

> Crown Him the Lord of years,
>   The Potentate of time;
> Creator of the rolling spheres,
>   Ineffably sublime.[1]

After nearly twenty long centuries a testimony cherished by members of the early Christian fellowship possesses a validity that has been vindicated by time: "Jesus Christ the same yesterday, and to-day, and for ever" (Heb. 13:8).

I

In our grievously shaken world we need the assurance which these words bring. Someone has said, "In a world that is all shook up, we need a Christianity that is unshaken and unshakable." But Christianity is no stranger to a world that is "all shook up." Its advent was in just such a world.

The little land in which Jesus was born had been for centuries a battle ground. Not only had the inhabitants engaged in civil strife, but their homeland had witnessed the struggles of Philistines, Assyrians, Egyptians, and Babylonians. Palestine had long been accustomed to tension, war, and revolution. The early years of the Christian era were particularly torn by the struggles of Jews and Romans which culminated in A.D. 63 when the imperial armies destroyed Jerusalem and fulfilled Jesus' prediction concerning the temple, "There shall not be left here one stone upon another, that shall not be thrown down" (Matt. 24:2). They wrongly read history who speak only of the serenity and peace of Galilee and think of Jesus as an anemic, pale Galilean.

Into a strife-torn world Jesus came with a gospel that had to prove

itself within the vortex of stress and tension. Did the word of Christ
meet the testings of that and later generations? Yes, indeed, for Christianity not only survived and grew in stature and influence but is
the most vital legacy of the ancient world to our times.

Here then is something unshakable that speaks with experience and
authority to our badly shaken world. We need to know Him who has
been and remains the supreme fact in life. Our generation desperately
needs His voice. If I mention only individual words, you will know
how changed and shaken our world is:

> ATOM BOMB
>
> HYDROGEN BOMB
>
> COBALT BOMB
>
> PUSH-BUTTON WAR
>
> GERM WARFARE
>
> COLD WAR
>
> SPACE WAR
>
> ICBM

Or if I speak of communism, you will know how shaken and divided
this world is. Even the word "democracy" also connotes upheaval for
many.

Some of the blessings of democracy, which we and our fathers before us took for granted, do not appeal to many of the world's dis-
tressed and distraught peoples. They have tried and rejected democracy, or they show neither interest nor inclination to follow the pattern
of government which we cherish.

A thoughtful church editor said to me:

You and I may wonder why democracy is not more readily accepted
and embraced by people in many other countries, but we tend to forget
that in this country we have been schooled in the democratic tradition
since childhood and they have not. In schoolrooms our small children
elect class officers. High school students vote for their May queens. You
and I have a vote in the selection of school officials. We practice democracy in our service clubs, our women's clubs, and churches. Our whole
lives are lived within a democratic context. But this has not been true of
much of the world. They have not been reared and trained in democracy,
and so they do not automatically accept the blessings of democracy as we
think they should.

A world that has been shaken needs a gospel that has withstood the changes of time, that has outlived every kind of government the minds of men can devise, and that has endured revolution, persecution, and trial by fire and sword. A world that has been shaken needs Jesus Christ, whose cross towers "o'er the wrecks of time."[2] Only he has "the words of eternal life" (John 6:68).

Some years ago the rulers in the Kremlin decided to publish a special edition of the writings of Stalin. This was to be a grand publication and in anticipation gold leaf to be used to emboss the cover was stored up in printing houses in East Germany. But, as must happen to all men of his kind, Stalin lost prestige and in a change of Kremlin policy his life and policies were deliberately downgraded. Then a strange and ironical thing happened, which is not without many parallels in Christian history. The Lutherans of East Germany petitioned their Communist overlords for permission to print Bibles for their spiritual brethren in the Baltic States and in Siberia. Not only was permission granted, but the gold leaf, collected to embellish the works of Stalin, was made available to the Lutherans for the bindings on their Bibles.

Is this strange, or is it an evidence of the power of God in history to make right the wrongs of men? Less than three centuries after the crucifixion of our Lord, the mortal enemy of Christianity, the Roman Empire, under Constantine the Great proclaimed the way of Christ to be the official religion of the children of the persecutors. Did not the home of Voltaire subsequently become the headquarters of the French Bible Society? Not Pilate nor Herod nor the pagan emperors of Rome nor Stalin is the supreme fact in history, but rather "Jesus Christ the same yesterday, and to-day, and for ever."

There is in *The Gauntlet* by James Street a moving scene in which an older and a younger preacher are conversing:

The old man went over to his bookcase and returned with his copy of *Life of Jesus*. He took off his shoes again as he sat down. "The skeptics enjoy quoting Renan because he picks fundamentalism to pieces." He wet his fingers and turned the pages. "However, the heart of any argument is found in its summation. Listen how Renan sums up his own findings." He held the book close to his good eye and read slowly:

" 'Mankind in its totality offers an assemblage of low beings, selfish, and superior to the animal only in that its selfishness is more reflective. From the midst of this uniform mediocrity, there are pillars that rise toward the sky, and bear witness to a nobler destiny. Jesus is the highest of these

pillars which show to man whence he comes, and whither he ought to
tend. In him was condensed all that is good and elevated in our nature.' "

The preacher's voice rose and fell. He pronounced each word distinctly.
There was something melodious in his reading voice. . . .

" 'Whatever may be the unexpected phenomena of the future, Jesus will
not be surpassed. His worship will constantly renew its youth, the tale of
his life will cause ceaseless tears, his sufferings will soften the best hearts;
all the ages will proclaim that, among the sons of men, there is none born
who is greater than Jesus.' "[3]

It would be well for us, especially those who have been Christians
for more years than they can remember, to learn more about the meaning of Jesus Christ as the supreme fact of life. We are not without
sufficient resources for knowing him. His is one of the best-attested
and most fully documented lives in history. We turn primarily to the
record of the Four Gospels. There we find revealed the timeless Christ.

> On Christ, the solid rock, I stand;
> All other ground is sinking sand.[4]

His life marks in more than one respect the dividing point in history.
Even those who deride and denounce him date their refutations according to the time of his birth! How may we better know him as the supreme fact in our own lives as well as in history?

II

We shall know and understand Jesus better when we accept him as
the supreme revelation of God to man. In a recent play a group of
soldiers are billeted in a church where their conversation turns almost
inevitably to the life of the spirit. Here is a snatch from their conversation:

DAVID: Allow me to make the introduction. God: man. Man: God.
ADAMS: I wish it could be so easy.[5]

The cry of Job, "Oh that I knew where I might find him!" (Job
23:3), has come from the lips of men of every generation. Thomas
Heywood, a seventeenth-century English poet, wrote:

> I askt the seas and all the deeps below
>   My God to know,
> I askt the reptiles, and whatever is
>   In the abyss;

> Even from the shrimps to the leviathan
> Enquiry ran;
> But in those deserts that no line can sound,
> The God I sought for was not to be found.[6]

And William Watson penned these lines:

> The God I know of, I shall ne'er
> Know, though he dwells exceeding nigh.
> *Raise thou the stone and find me there,*
> *Cleave thou the wood and there am I.*
> Yea, in my flesh his spirit doth flow,
> Too near, too far, for me to know.[7]

But he for whom all men have sought is revealed in Jesus Christ. Here is the biblical witness of this matchless truth:

They shall call his name Emmanuel, which being interpreted is, God with us (Matt. 1:23).
For in him dwelleth all the fulness of the Godhead bodily (Col. 2:9).
He that hath seen me hath seen the Father (John 14:9).
I am come in my Father's name (John 5:43).
The Word was made flesh, and dwelt among us (John 1:14).
God was in Christ, reconciling the world unto himself (2 Cor. 5:19).
God was manifest in the flesh, justified in the Spirit, seen of angels, preached unto the Gentiles, believed on in the world, received up into glory (1 Tim. 3:16).

The people of my home state Virginia have a heritage of which they are justly proud. They claim, for instance, in

> Fairfax County that Washington slept here,
> Albemarle County that Jefferson lived here, and
> Westmoreland County that Robert E. Lee was born here.

But great as these honors are they diminish when we realize that

> Bethlehem may claim God was born here,
> Nazareth that God labored here,
> Galilee that God taught here,
> Bethany that God rested here,
> Gethsemane that God prayed here,
> Golgotha that God died here, and
> Joseph's Garden that God rose here.

This doctrine that Deity humbled himself, was made in the likeness of men, was born a babe in Bethlehem, was crucified upon a cross that all of the fullness of God might be revealed, is called the Incarnation. This is a doctrine which spells out for all men to understand that the eternal nature of God is love: "For God so loved the world, that he gave his only begotten Son, that whosoever believeth in him should not perish, but have everlasting life" (John 3:16).

We shall never fully understand or appreciate the blessing of the Incarnation until we think of how limited our knowledge of God would be apart from the life and teaching of Jesus Christ. Something of the necessity of Christ's role as mediator between God and man is found in this discussion from a novel that was widely read a generation or so ago:

> Jolly looked at his father.
> "Do you believe in God, Dad? I've never known." . . . .
> "What do you mean by God?" he said; "there are two irreconcilable ideas of God. There's the Unknowable Creative Principle—one believes in That. And there's the Sum of altruism in man—naturally one believes in That."
> "I see. That leaves out Christ, doesn't it?"
> Jolyon stared. Christ, the link between those two ideas! Out of the mouth of babes! Here was orthodoxy scientifically explained at last! The sublime poem of the Christ life was man's attempt to join those two irreconcilable conceptions of God. And since the Sum of human altruism was as much a part of the Unknowable Creative Principle as anything else in Nature and the Universe, a worse link might have been chosen after all   Funny— how one went through life without seeing it in that sort of way![8]

The Incarnation, this linking of the apparently irreconcilable natures of the divine and the human, is a gift to undeserving men because of the prodigality of God's love and grace. Our only appropriate posture is one of humility. If you wish to enter the Church of the Nativity in Bethlehem, the site traditionally given as the place of our Lord's birth, you must bow low in order to pass through the little door.

> Where meek souls will receive Him still,
> The dear Christ enters in.[9]

How blessed are those who find this to be true! A young woman who had been hoodwinked by materialism and atheism found life with her husband so filled with depression and bitterness that both she and he saw only a bleak and bare future. But then something glorious happened. "All of a sudden God came in!" she later said. They became

Christians, and their lives, home, and mutual relationship were transformed. She told of their experience in these words: "Only One sums up so much of what God means, and that One is Jesus Christ." Even now as of old those who open their hearts to Christ will receive his promise: "Behold, I stand at the door, and knock: if any man hear my voice, and open the door, I will come in to him, and will sup with him, and he with me" (Rev. 3:20). Then shall we know that Jesus Christ is the supreme fact in life because he reveals God to us.

III

We may know Jesus as the supreme fact in life, secondly, because *he reveals man at his best.* He shows us what man may be when his life is imbued with the grace and the love of God. He shows us persuasively for he is our perfect example from the past, our best guide for the present, and our living hope for the future.

Pilate said, "I find no fault in this man" (Luke 23:4). Since that far distant day, men have again and again said the same thing about him. Men have tried to outrival one another in claiming perfection for him. We do not speak of anyone else with the superlatives we heap upon Jesus. Even the most indulgent wife does not claim perfection for her husband. Loving parents do not blind themselves to the weakness of their children. Our heroes—and most people are hero-worshipers—have hands and feet of clay. Not so with Jesus! One of the most eloquent tributes to Christ came from a Southern poet, Sidney Lanier:

> But Thee, but Thee, O sovereign Seer of Time,
> But Thee, O poet's Poet, Wisdom's Tongue,
> But Thee, O man's best Man, O love's best Love,
> O perfect life in perfect labor writ,
> O all men's Comrade, Servant, King, or Priest—
> What *if* and *yet*, what mole, what flaw, what lapse,
> What least defect or shadow of defect,
> What rumor, tattled by an enemy,
> Of inference loose, what lack of grace
> Even in torture's grasp, or sleep's or death's—
> Oh, what amiss may I forgive in Thee,
> Jesus, good Paragon, thou Crystal Christ?[10]

Because of Jesus we may take heart, knowing that he has given "us an example, that [we] should follow his steps" (1 Pet. 2:21). We

may take hope, for we see in him what a man can be like if he strives
to be like Jesus. We may take confident assurance that we can grow
more and more like him even in a shaken, troubled world and in the
face of temptation and trial.

"The Mark of the Hawk," a motion picture produced by one of
our American denominations, is the story of the struggle between white
and black men in an African country. One of the native terrorist groups
has taken the hawk as the sign of their displeasure. A dead hawk is
hung on the door of any family or individual which the group has
marked for destruction.

A Christian missionary, attempting to mediate between the whites
and the blacks, confronts the leader of the terrorist band. This man,
who has known the Christian faith but has turned from it, upbraids
the missionary by saying that he was thrown out of China and now
will be put out of Africa. But the missionary tells the native leader
that in China he and his wife had adopted a Chinese boy, who grew
up as a Christian in a happy home. Then the Communists came. They
drafted the boy into the army and tortured and imprisoned the missionary. One day the Communists sent the boy, now partially brain-
washed, to his father's cell. The boy denounced his father, but the
father said, "Son, I have failed you, but Christ did not fail you. The
greatest gift one man can give another is Jesus Christ, and I have given
Jesus to you. Whatever may happen, remember that with Christ I am
never alone, for we are more than conquerors through him who loved
us."

At this point the boy broke down, renewed his Christian faith, and
resolved to be a Christian at whatever cost—and it would be costly.
When the Communist officers learned what had happened, they took
the boy away to be shot as a collaborator. His father called after him,
"Remember, we are more than conquerors," and the boy replied,
"Through him who loved us."

This story deeply moves the black leader, and he too reaffirms his
faith in Christ. Together the missionary and the native leader attempt
to ward off a raid of the black against the white. In the struggle the
missionary is mortally wounded. As he is dying, he looks up and says,
"We are more than conquerors." "Yes," replies his black brother,
"through him who loved us."

The supreme hope for our troubled generation lies with yellow, white, and black men who strive to live and live together according to the example of Jesus Christ.

Is Jesus the supreme fact in *your* life? Do you test your attitudes and actions by asking, "What would Jesus say? What would Jesus do? How would Jesus meet this or that situation? How would Jesus handle this problem?" When we permit him to guide and direct us, he will become the supreme fact in our lives and our world will be the better for it.

9.

How to Live a New Kind of Life

IN HER REMARKABLE BOOK, *The Savage My Kinsman,* Elisabeth Elliot records vividly the story of her mission to the Auca Indians in Ecuador. What makes this a particularly heart-throbbing chronicle is the fact that these were the very same Indians who had earlier killed her husband and his four missionary companions. Yet she possessed a deep sense of commitment to her husband's unfinished work and to her Lord. Was she fearful and apprehensive? She was strengthened in the remembrance of the words of Paul: "We can enlighten men only because we can give them knowledge of the glory of God, as we see it in the face of Jesus Christ" (2 Cor. 4:6, PHILLIPS).

What she faced when living with uncivilized Indians in their great open huts was something her reading, study, and previous thought had hardly prepared her for. She was forced to reappraise her whole life and her concept of missionary work. These people had almost nothing in common with her. Judged by the standards to which she was accustomed, theirs was a crude and hard life. Yet her thinking was dominated by the overriding conviction that she must attempt to communicate to them the most precious thing she knew. Her mission is expressed in this moving sentence: "We must live with them, love

66

them, try to understand them, and above all, demonstrate to them what we meant by eternal life: a new *kind* of life, not simply a longer one."[1]

Christianity is a new kind of life. Jesus said, "I am come that they might have life, and that they might have it more abundantly" (John 10:10). Two recent translations render this verse as follows: "I have come that they may have life and have it to the full" (MOFFATT) and "I came to bring them life, and far more life than before" (PHILLIPS). Those who truly know Jesus can testify to what it means to have "far more life than before" and to experience life "to the full."

I

What is new about this kind of life? It begins with *a new birth*. Just as we were once born physically, so must we be born again spiritually. "That which is born of the flesh is flesh," Jesus told Nicodemus, "and that which is born of the Spirit is spirit" (John 3:6). This second birth, which the Apostle Paul called "newness of life" (Rom. 6:4), is essential if a man is to "enter into the kingdom of God" (John 3:5). It comes as a consequence of the conscious choice of the believer and brings forgiveness of sin, release from guilt and fear, and the joyousness found only in a wholly new way of life.

The new life is lived by *a new creature*. "If any man be in Christ, he is a new creature: old things are passed away; behold, all things are become new" (2 Cor. 5:17). In *Mr. Britling Sees It Through*, a novel by H. G. Wells that was widely read during World War I, is portrayed the importance of the Creator to those whom he in love created:

Religion is the first thing and the last thing, and until a man has found God and been found by God, he begins at no beginning, he works to no end. He may have his friendships, his partial loyalties, his scraps of honour. But all these things fall into place and life falls into place only with God. Only with God. God, who fights through men against Blind Force and Night and Non-Existence; who is the end, who is the meaning.[2]

How fittingly the Christian sings:

What a wonderful change in my life has been wrought,
Since Jesus came into my heart!

> I have light in my soul for which long I have sought,
>   Since Jesus came into my heart![3]

The believer lives with *a new faith*. He learns to "walk by faith, not by sight" (2 Cor. 5:7).

> Columbus found a world, and had no chart
> Save one that faith deciphered in the skies;
> To trust the soul's invincible surmise
> Was all his science and his only art.[4]

So deeply impressed was Martin Luther by this faith that transcends sight that he adopted as the text of his life and theology the simple phrase, "The just shall live by faith" (Rom. 1:17). The believer's faith has a wide arc, for his faith in God includes also faith in other men and ultimately faith in himself as an instrument of God.

To the believer in Christ comes *a new hope*. Though he must walk —as indeed every man does—through the valley of the shadow, he sorrows not as one who has no hope. To hope in God simply means to trust in God for life here and hereafter. The Christian confidently faces the future, for his trust is lodged in One who is far greater than himself. Many have learned the quiet lesson of which Whittier writes:

> I know not what the future hath
>   Of marvel or surprise,
> Assured alone that life and death
>   His mercy underlies.
>
> *
>
> I know not where His islands lift
>   Their fronded palms in air;
> I only know I cannot drift
>   Beyond His love and care.[5]

This life is characterized by *a new love*. When Paul found the transforming power of love in Christ, he despised those things he had formerly loved and loved that which he had formerly hated. This is no ordinary human love but a new love whose standard and measure are uplifted by divine grace.

Love was the keystone in the life of Jesus. He said, "As the Father hath loved me, so have I loved you. . . . This is my commandment, That ye love one another, as I have loved you" (John 15:9, 12). "Herein is love, not that we loved God, but that he loved us. . . . Beloved, if God so loved us, we ought also to love one another" (1

John 4:10-11). And not only those who are easy to love, but those who are unlovely and unlovable, for "if ye love them which love you, what reward have ye?" (Matt. 5:46).

All of this new kind of life is lived with *a new perspective*. We are called to be citizens of heaven. Paul wrote to the Philippians, "We are a colony of heaven" (Phil. 3:20, MOFFATT). We live not for today only but in the assurance that we shall "ever be with the Lord" (1 Thess. 4:17). The vision of the world-to-be challenges the believer to give himself in devoted service to that day when there shall be a "new heaven and a new earth, wherein dwelleth righteousness" (2 Pet. 3:13).

To this new perspective is added *a new purpose*. In the synagogue at Nazareth, Jesus indicated the nature of his mission by quoting from Isaiah:

> The Spirit of the Lord is upon me, because he hath anointed me to preach the gospel to the poor; he hath sent me to heal the brokenhearted, to preach deliverance to the captives, and recovering of sight to the blind, to set at liberty them that are bruised, to preach the acceptable year of the Lord.
>
> Luke 4:18-19

Jesus bestows upon each of us a legacy and a *raison d'être,* a reason or justification for our existence. What is this? To give the gospel to the world.

> We've a story to tell to the nations
> That shall turn their hearts to the right,
> A story of truth and mercy,
> A story of peace and light.[6]

Was any generation of men ever confronted with more of an opportunity to bring truth, mercy, peace, and light to a hard and crusty people who have known little more than illusion, alarums of war, and the shadow of doubt and despair? It behooves a Christian to work while it is still day and also to respond to that "holy calling, not according to our works, but according to [God's] own purpose and grace" (2 Tim. 1:9). For we labor not for ourselves but for the Eternal, and our devotion to him is best attested to by the manner in which we emulate "the eternal purpose which he purposed in Christ Jesus our Lord" (Eph. 3:11). In his Second Inaugural Address, Lincoln said,

"The Almighty has his own purposes." Later he wrote, "Men are not flattered by being shown that there has been a difference of purpose between the Almighty and them."[7] Dominated by a purpose that transcends our commonplace aims and motives, we may say with Paul, "To me to live is Christ, and to die is gain" (Phil. 1:21), and to sing with Frances R. Havergal:

> Take my will, and make it Thine;
> It shall be no longer mine.

Finally, the new kind of life brings *a new sense of values*. A value is that to which we ascribe excellence and intrinsic worth. The Christian most values treasures in heaven. He looks "not at the things which are seen, but at the things which are not seen: for the things which are seen are temporal; but the things which are not seen are eternal" (2 Cor. 4:18).

Pat Neff, one-time governor of Texas, came to realize, as he often said, that if he hoped to have treasures in heaven, then he must center his thoughts and efforts in that which is heavenly. He bade farewell to politics, gave himself unreservedly to youth, and served for many years as president of Baylor University. In his commitment to youth he found those values which infuse life here with joy and meaning and also have eternal significance.

II

Having considered what is new in this new kind of life, let us think of the qualities which, like the golden threads in a tapestry, are woven into this new life in Christ.

First, there is the fact that this life is *everlasting*. The focus of the Christian is the distant horizon where he will one day enjoy the nearer presence of God. "We know that if our earthly house of this tabernacle were dissolved, we have a building of God, an house not made with hands, eternal in the heavens" (2 Cor. 5:1). Our Christ is the Lord of life who "hath abolished death, and hath brought life and immortality to light through the gospel" (2 Tim. 1:10). In all things we "are more than conquerors through him that loved us" (Rom. 8:37).

The believer treasures the assurance of immortality, but eternal life is far more than just living on and on and on. Eternal life is that quality of life which comes with conversion and is worthy of everlasting perpetuation. The ordinary significance of chronological time is shattered, for eternal life begins now and spans all time. The believer is bilingual, for even as he is learning the language of heaven he speaks the diction of this world where God has given him a noble work to do in His name. In this work the believer discerns a foretaste of that greater glory.

The second quality of this new life is that it is *expanding*. In company with his Master, the Christian grows. He seeks always better to know the mind of Christ. His faith matures as he tests it, lives by its precepts, and finds it to be true. There is a geometric progression in the Christian life, and to each rewarding experience is added a multitude of richer experiences.

> Build thee more stately mansions, O my soul,
> As the swift seasons roll!
> Leave thy low-vaulted past!
> Let each new temple, nobler than the last,
> Shut thee from heaven with a dome more vast,
> Till thou at length are free,
> Leaving thine outgrown shell by life's
> unresting sea![8]

Note the expanding life that the early Christians were challenged to make their own:

> Add to your faith virtue;
> and to virtue knowledge;
> and to knowledge temperance;
> and to temperance patience;
> and to patience godliness;
> and to godliness brotherly kindness;
> and to brotherly kindness charity.
> 2 Pet. 1:5-7

We read that the boy Jesus "increased in wisdom and stature, and in favour with God and man" (Luke 2:52). At last from a cross raised on a hill outside of Jerusalem Jesus demonstrated unforgettably how his heart embraced in love all mankind.

Thirdly, this new life is *exemplary*. A true believer is dependable. One knows how he will meet a situation, whether it be a temptation or a tragedy, for he is schooled in discipline, renunciation, and self-denial. He seeks, insofar as God strengthens his will, to live according to the injunction of Paul: "Whatsoever things are

> honest. . .
> just. . .
> pure. . .
> lovely. . .
> of good report;
> if there be any virtue, and
> if there be any praise,
> think on these things."
>
> Phil. 4:8

A young serviceman kept near his bunk a small copy of a portrait of Jesus Christ. The picture was a constant reminder of an invisible companionship and seemed to say, though in silent eloquence, to everyone who entered the barracks: "He and I live here together. Because of My presence, you know what to expect of him. There are some things which for My sake he will not say nor do. There are other things you can always count on him to do and to stand for."

Fourthly, in this new kind of life the believer is *expendable*. With his Lord whom he loves and serves, he says, "For their sakes I sanctify myself" (John 17:19). He knows the meaning and implications of Christ's teaching, "Greater love hath no man than this, that a man lay down his life for his friends" (John 15:13).

Our mortal lives are precious to us, and we do not willingly surrender them except to that which we most covet and cherish. When the Roman captain asks Lavinia, a young Christian in Shaw's play, why she is willing to die as a martyr, she replies:

I don't know. If it were for anything small enough to know, it would be too small to die for. I think I'm going to die for God. Nothing else is real enough to die for.[9]

The honor roll of God's expendables is "an endless line of splendor."[10] Through the long Christian centuries and in our own day, men and women have joyously given themselves for the sake of Christ and the gospel.

Dr. William Wallace, who had served as a medical missionary in

China for many years, resolved to stay at his hospital and continue his ministry of healing even after the Communists came. So devoted and sacrificial was his loyalty to God and the people that the Communists decided they would have to destroy him. His daily life and witness undercut all the lies and propaganda they were spreading concerning the West. So they imprisoned him on trumped-up charges. Then one day his friends were notified that he had died in prison and that they should prepare his body for burial. "What shall we put on the grave marker?" the missionaries asked the Chinese Christians. His grave inscription, the one which they considered to be most singularly appropriate, reads:

FOR ME TO LIVE IS CHRIST.

Such individuals bear witness to the inescapable requirement which Christ places upon his followers. May we never neglect nor forget their witness. In Maxwell Anderson's play, *Valley Forge,* Washington speaks of those who gave their last full measure of devotion for American independence.

This liberty will look easy by and by
when nobody dies to get it.[11]

We constantly find inspiration and challenge in those who in Christ's name shouldered their crosses and spent and were spent.

More frequently, however, you and I are called, not to die for Christ, but to live for him. Opportunities for sacrificial and devoted service are part of our day-by-day experience in home and business and week-by-week in the church.

At a summer assembly a young mother cared for her own three boys and for twenty other children from her church. In the morning she prepared breakfast for the live-wire children, she shepherded them during Bible study and play, and at night she fed them before tucking them in bed. She gave all she had to those youngsters. When I saw her engaged in this tremendously demanding and arduous labor, I thought of what Christ said: "Inasmuch as ye have done it unto one of the least of these my brethren, ye have done it unto me" (Matt. 25:40). Her wisdom, patience, and devotion to Christ are indelibly inscribed on the hearts of those boys and girls. Who would say that her service is less important in the economy of the Kingdom than that of some heroic trailblazer in the vanguard of Christian missions?

Fifthly, this new life is *exhilarating*. Nothing quite equals the radiant stimulation and joy of the Christian life. Those who long ago did not understand the spontaneous gladness of the early Christians thought that they were mad, beside themselves, and intoxicated at midmorning (Acts 2:13-15). Little did they comprehend the words of Jesus: "These things have I spoken unto you, that my joy might remain in you, and that your joy might be full" (John 15:11). But the believer knows that this wide world offers no deeper and more abiding satisfaction than to be a pioneer for Christ, to stand vigorously and valiantly for right and truth, and to invest even the last portion of his time and talent in that which he knows to be the supreme good.

When asked if it were not thrilling to create a statue, a great sculptor answered, "The statue was there all the time. I merely chipped away the unwanted stone." This, of course, oversimplifies the creative genius of the artist, and yet the Christian knows that when he puts his life into the hands of the Master, the old self will be chipped away and the true man will emerge.

III

Do you know this new kind of life? Through faith and commitment, it may be yours. It will not be easy and it may cost heavily, but to live by faith is at last to learn that

> It makes the coward spirit brave,
> And nerves the feeble arm for fight;
> It takes the terror from the grave,
> And gilds the bed of death with light.[12]

If you wish to stake your personal claim on this new kind of life, don't necessarily head for the hills or for the city or book passage for a foreign mission station. Start where you are. It is said of Henry David Thoreau that when a visitor in Concord, Massachusetts, asked him if there were Indian arrowheads thereabouts, Henry, by way of answering, bent over and picked up one from the dust. There are "acres of diamonds" to be mined in your own home, neighborhood, and church. To live the abundant life Christ promised, begin today at the place where God has put you. Even there you will discover the glorious difference Christ makes.

Elisabeth Elliot writes of the time when an Auca woman ordered her to bring a clay pot:

> It was my pot but I took it to her. "Well—don't bring it *empty*. Go get some water in it."
> I had to go down to the river by means of a log which lay at a steep angle, fill the pot, and carry it (it had no handles and was very heavy) back up the slippery log. The old woman took it without a word.[13]

But joy filled her heart. She had been accepted. She was one with them, but even more, she realized that she was at one with her Lord who said, "The servant is not greater than his lord; neither he that is sent greater than he that sent him" (John 13:16). "I am among you as he that serveth" (Luke 22:27).

Jesus says to each of us what he said to his disciples long ago: "If any man will come after me, let him deny himself, and take up his cross, and follow me" (Matt. 16:24). Do this, give your heart to it unreservedly, and you too will find the everlasting joy of a new kind of life.

10.

How to Become a Better Christian

AN IRATE YOUNG MAN, whose Christian idealism had not been worn smooth by compromise and conformity, stormed into my study. "Why are they all like that?" he asked. His manner was stern, but I knew that underneath he was deeply troubled. We had often talked on topics dealing with the Christian life.

"Why are who like what?" I queried.

"Christians!" he exclaimed. "Why are they like that?"

"Like what?"

"Why don't they act Christian in their relations with other people?"

"A very good question." I told him, "and one that I have asked myself repeatedly." We talked about what being a Christian means and of so-called Christians who are too satisfied even to move from their pious ruts and also of Christians who are dissatisfied but do nothing. Then I reminded him of mutual friends in whom the spirit of our Lord is incarnate and who are radiant witnesses of Christ in home, church, and community. I quoted Browning's familiar words:

> Ah, but a man's reach should exceed his grasp,
> Or what's a heaven for?[1]

The perfection to which our Lord calls us always seems elusive and beyond our most earnest and consecrated efforts.

76

The young man brought an end to our conversation by making this request: "Please preach a sermon on the unchristian things that Christian people do." I said that every sermon included this and that it is incumbent on present-day preachers, as it was for the ancient prophets, to summon men and women to the "high calling of God in Christ Jesus" (Phil. 3:14).

The protestation of my youthful friend raises two questions: What is involved in becoming a Christian? and What are the things that are becoming in a Christian?

Actually, a man may become a Christian in a twinkling of an eye. At the very moment he confesses his sins, repents, and accepts Jesus as Savior, he is a new man in Christ and a Christian. He is, as our Lord instructed Nicodemus, "born again" (John 3:7). This is the imperative first step but only the first. One pastor tells of a lovely and lovable older woman who was told by a young woman, "You are truly a beautiful person." Her reply was, "I should be, for I am seventy years old." When we speak of what it means to become a Christian, we should not overlook the other side of the coin, which is the character and way of life that is becoming in a Christian.

How can we live worthily as Christ's disciples? How can we do those things that are pleasing to him and will make us pleasing to others? How in the face of difficulties can we do the fitting and proper thing and so measure up to all that we expect of ourselves as Christians and that others expect of us as members of the body of Christ? How can we grow in faith until we attain "the stature of the fulness of Christ" (Eph. 4:13)?

John records in his generation an answer which is equally true for Christians today: "As many as received him, to them gave he power to become the sons of God" (John 1:12). We need to grow "in grace, and in the knowledge of our Lord and Saviour Jesus Christ" (2 Pet. 3:18). Becoming a Christian requires changes in life. Like Paul, we must "put away childish things" (1 Cor. 13:11).

I

First, becoming a Christian does not mean merely that *we get something,* though, of course, we do. Salvation is given to us. "By grace are ye saved through faith; and that not of yourselves: it is the gift of God" (Eph. 2:8). Salvation brings forgiveness of sin, cleansing from unrighteousness, inner peace, and a new life of assurance and hope. These blessings come when we choose with God's help to commit ourselves to live as Christ would have us.

By becoming a follower of Christ, we get the name "Christian" and get our names on a church roll. But to make that name and membership meaningful, we need help and power from beyond ourselves. Søren Kierkegaard, the Danish philosopher and theologian, wrote of a man who, searching the streets of a strange city for a laundry, finally found a store window in which was a sign reading:

LAUNDRY DONE HERE.

Taking his dirty clothes into the store, he asked, "When can I have these clothes back?" The astounded man to whom he spoke said, "What do you mean? We don't do laundry. We paint signs." We bear the name "Christian," but do our lives measure up to the profession we make? To claim the name "Christian," important though that is, is not enough.

Secondly, becoming a Christian also means more than that *we learn something*, though, of course, we do. Christ said, "Learn of me" (Matt. 11:29). Within the classroom of Christ we are taught that "whatsoever things were written aforetime were written for our learning" (Rom. 15:4). It is needful for us as Christians to study the Bible, the Word of God. We shall never exhaust the truths to be found within its pages. These truths will set us free from bondage to sin, fear, and death and bring us love and joy, mercy and peace, strength and courage.

A former parishioner writes me of the wonderful things she has been doing since becoming a Christian and of the joy she finds in Christian service. She closed one letter with these words: "Whoever would have thought such things would happen to me? I used to be such a little mouse. I am now an entirely different person." She is learning what it means to be a Christian.

Thirdly, becoming a Christian does not mean only that *we do something*, although the Christian life does call us to action. "Lord, and what shall this man do?" (John 21:21). We are "under orders." Like the first disciples, we "cannot but speak the things which we have seen and heard" (Acts 4:20). Our call is to action in the world-wide struggle of beliefs. We are called to build up Christ's church and to advance the Kingdom of God in the hearts of men. The Scriptures truly say, "Faith, if it hath not works, is dead" (Jas. 2:17). The rich young ruler failed at this point. Jesus told him that he must do something—sell his goods for the benefit of the poor and then follow him. The young man was unprepared to go that far—and he wandered off into spiritual oblivion.

Fourthly, becoming a Christian surely means that *we give something*. Even as the Macedonian Christians "first gave their own selves to the Lord" (2 Cor. 8:5), so must we. And also our money, our time, and our talents, according as God has blessed us. After Jean Valjean had stolen from the priest who had befriended him in Victor Hugo's novel, the police apprehended and returned him. But the priest, instead of pressing charges, gave Jean the candlesticks, saying that he had forgotten them. After the police had left, the priest said to Jean, "Remember, life is to give and not to take."[2] We are to give, even as God for Christ's sake has given to us.

> Laid on thine altar, O my Lord divine,
>   Accept this gift today for Jesus' sake;
> I have no jewels to adorn thy shrine,
>   No far-famed sacrifice to make;
> But here within my trembling hand I bring
>   This will of mine—a thing that seemeth small.
> But thou alone, O Lord, canst understand
>   How when I yield thee this, I yield mine all.[3]

Fifthly, becoming a Christian means that *we be something*. "If any man be in Christ, he is a new creature: old things are passed away; behold, all things are become new" (2 Cor. 5:17). We become different persons as we grow more and more like our Master. And beyond this, we become "witnesses unto me both in Jerusalem, and in all Judaea, and in Samaria, and unto the uttermost part of the earth" (Acts 1:8). What kind of witness can we be? Does our witness help or hinder the cause of Christ?

A beautiful monument on the campus of Oberlin College commemorates those who gave their lives during the Boxer uprising in China at the turn of the century. Above the honor roll are these words:

NOT THAT I COUNT MY LIFE DEAR UNTO MYSELF.

At the center of the monument, carved into red marble, is the following:

YE ARE WITNESSES.

We too are witnesses to all that God in Christ has done for us.

II

How may we, who have become Christians, achieve that witness which is becoming to Christians? The doorway of understanding is opened by the affirmation of the fourth Evangelist, "As many as received him, to them gave he power to become the sons of God" (John 1:12]. In an age of power we need this greater power. We human beings, who have watched the remarkable movement from manpower to horsepower to atomic power, need to remember that the Source of all power will provide the strength essential for endeavor in the realm of the Spirit.

Not only must we use wisely the physical power entrusted to us, but we must claim the promised spiritual power so that we may be "strengthened with might by his Spirit in the inner man" (Eph. 3:16). We need also the mental power that comes when we have "the mind of Christ" (1 Cor. 2:16) and the personal power that comes with the assurance that "I am with you alway" (Matt. 28:20). Only by receiving this power may we say with Paul, "I can do all things through Christ which strengtheneth me" (Phil. 4:13).

This power must serve a purpose beyond ourselves. Our powers must be so disciplined, controlled, and directed that we become worthy and useful servants of the Kingdom. Only in this way shall we achieve and retain truth, freedom, and man's other precious rights.

Just think what such an achievement means! After two Frenchmen in 1950 scaled the heights of Annapurna in the Nepal Himalayas, James Ramsey Ullman wrote:

> There are still among us those who are willing to struggle greatly and suffer greatly for wholly ideal ends; for whom security is not the be-all and end-all of living; for whom there are conquests to be won in the world other than over their fellow men.[4]

And Maurice Herzog, whose toes and fingers, frozen during that ascent, were later amputated, wrote:

> Together we knew toil, joy and pain. . . . In my worst moments of anguish . . . I saw that it was better to be true than to be strong. The marks of the ordeal are apparent on my body. I was saved and I had won my freedom. This freedom, which I shall never lose, has given me the assurance and serenity of a man who has fulfilled himself.[5]

Christ has promised divine assistance—spiritual power—to those who seek Christian fulfillment. But first we must make a personal decision to receive him and believe in him.

A small boy had long been a problem pupil. Then one day a new teacher, who was a devout Christian, established with the boy a genuine understanding based on mutual trust and friendliness. When parents were invited to see an exhibition of the children's work, the boy watched nervously as his own parents picked up his copybook. He had reason for being apprehensive, for he had spoiled many pages by writing mocking comments and drawing caricatures of his other teachers, although in the later pages he had tried to show himself as a better student. Imagine his amazement when his parents turned from one page to the next and showed delight in all they saw. Then the boy realized that his teacher had removed the spoiled pages. Later when he was alone with his teacher, the boy asked why she had done this. The teacher's answer left an imperishable mark on the life of the youngster. "Do you know who taught me to do that?" she asked. "It was Jesus. He did just that for me. He removed from my life all that was evil and unworthy and has helped me to do what is right. Let him do that for you."[6]

And he will! Through him we are empowered both to become Christian and to do those things that are becoming in Christians.

11.

How to Be Found Faithful with Life

THE YEAR IS A.D. 50 or thereabouts. The place is the home of a Christian in Ephesus. The man is the Apostle Paul. The occasion is the reporting to the Apostle of moral corruption and unchristian behavior within the Christian fellowship in Corinth. As a consequence the Apostle begins to write or perhaps to dictate a letter to the members of the Corinthian church.

In his mind the Apostle visualizes one by one the Corinthian Christians. They were his children in Christ. Their church was the fruit of eighteen months of labor in the Greek city of some half million or more inhabitants.

He understands their feeble human nature and knows that sin and temptation press in upon his children whose identity as Christians is daily threatened by exposure to wickedness which had long since made Corinth infamous in the Mediterranean world. Had his heart not been thrilled as he stood atop the Acrocorinth and viewed from that eighteen-thousand-foot vantage point a view of breathtaking majesty? And had not his spirits sunk within him as he looked down upon the great bronze statue of Athena, symbolic of wickedness that had corrupted the city to its very core?

In the home of an Ephesian friend, the Apostle determines to write a letter which will reprimand the faithlessness of the Christian brethren in Corinth. Yet his words must be seasoned with the inspiring harmonies of Christian love. From his great heart that in love and devotion spans the broad Aegean Sea comes this message: "It is required in stewards, that a man be found faithful" (1 Cor. 4:2). I particularly like the emphasis of Dr. Phillips' translation: "It is a prime requisite in a trustee that he should prove worthy of his trust."

We Christians of the latter half of the twentieth century, no less than the Corinthians of the first century, are required to be faithful. We are entrusted with worship, administration, prayer, world vision and witness, and fundamental Christian convictions. Basic, of course, to all of our responsibilities is our faithfulness not only *in life* but also *with life*. Only as we are faithful with life can we be faithful in all of the other important aspects of our Christian commitment.

Each of us has but one life to live. How best can we use it to the glory of God?

> But once I pass this way,
> And then—no more.
> But once—and then, the Silent Door
> Swings on its hinges,—
> Opens . . . . . . closes,—
> And no more
> I pass this way.
> So while I may,
> With all my might,
> I will essay
> Sweet comfort and delight,
> To all I meet upon the Pilgrim Way.
> For no man travels twice
> The Great Highway,
> That climbs through Darkness up to Light,—
> Through Night
> To Day.[1]

How precious life is to each of us! We have only one life to live, and it is soon ended. When our lives are charged with a sense of mission, the words of Nathan Hale seem particularly poignant: "I regret that I have but one life to give for my country." "For what is your life? It is even a vapour, that appeareth for a little time, and then vanisheth away" (Jas. 4:14). A stoic truth with which no man can quarrel!

Because we have only "threescore years and ten" (Ps. 90:10)—
give or take a little according as health and the exigencies of life permit—we must make every effort to realize life's fullest potential. With
God's help we can, for he can bring wonderful results into any life that
is found faithful. Dr. Courts Redford recalls that as a boy he was weak,
shy, and unduly self-critical. Then one day a loved one said, "Courts,
you are God's boy. He is not going to permit anything to happen to
you that you cannot handle." These words were like spiritual vitamins
and, as Dr. Redford later said, "They changed my life." He kept faith
with God and God with him, and a rich Christian ministry has followed.

To be found faithful with life we need to learn from Jesus this fundamental truth: "Whosoever will save his life shall lose it; but whosoever shall lose his life for my sake and the gospel's, the same shall
save it" (Mark 8:35). This matter of losing and saving life involves
a number of basic ideas, which can be interpreted in a simple formula.
Throughout my life as a pastor and counselor I have tried to reduce
my ideas to an A B C pattern which I might count off on the fingers
of my hand.

First, to be found faithful with life you must *accept your life* as
God's gift. Perhaps your life is not all you might wish, and you may
feel sometimes that life has shortchanged you, giving talents to others
which have been denied to you. But you are not responsible for the
talents of others, nor are you called to be faithful with what God has
given them.

Our responsibility is to use for the glory of God what he has given
to us. Remember that each life is a gift of God, and always life is
more than the body, raiment, or talents.

Dr. Ralph W. Sockman speaks of an old friend who, after earning a
doctorate in philosophy at Columbia University, served for many
years as a Christian missionary in China. The guiding prayer of his
life was, "O God, our Father, I accept thy gift of life. Help me to pass
it on for Jesus' sake." Before his death at the age of ninety-two, he
voiced another secret of his long and faithful life: "If we live the eternal life now, we will always."

Secondly, to be found faithful with life you must *better your life* so
that its richest possibilities may be realized. We are called to "grow in
grace, and in the knowledge of our Lord and Savior Jesus Christ" (2

Pet. 3:18). In his commission, "Ye shall be witnesses unto me" (Acts 1:8), Jesus places upon us a heavy and vital responsibility. We could not possibly measure up to that challenge did he not couple with the commission his promise, "Ye shall receive power, after that the Holy Ghost is come upon you." How spiritually energizing it is to know that when we want to better our lives God is ready and able to help us and that he will meet any life at any time at its point of deepest need! Little wonder that we love to sing these words of confident trust:

> I look to Thee in every need,
>   And never look in vain;
> I feel Thy strong and tender love,
>   And all is well again.[2]

The Psalmist expresses a similar sentiment: "Whither shall I go from thy spirit? or whither shall I flee from thy presence? . . . If I take the wings of the morning, and dwell in the uttermost parts of the sea; even there shall thy hand lead me, and thy right hand shall hold me" (Ps. 139:7, 9-10).

What we in our own strength are unable to do, we can accomplish through the grace and power of the living Christ. He accepts us as we are—our weaknesses, scars, and stains of sin—and helps us to be what we ought to be.

In a great shipyard I watched workmen cut a weak spot from a steel casting and weld in its place a new piece. After this casting had passed through the annealing process, it was stronger than ever. If we wish truly to better our lives, the Lord Jesus will

> Take from our souls the strain and stress,
> And let our ordered lives confess
>   The beauty of [His] peace.[3]

Thirdly, to be found faithful with life you must *consecrate your life*. Our stewardship of life is predicated upon our commitment to Christ's Kingdom. "Commit thy way unto the Lord; trust also in him; and he shall bring it to pass" (Ps. 37:5). "In all thy ways acknowledge him, and he shall direct thy paths" (Prov. 3:6). Without such a commitment, life is devoid of direction, emphasis, and power.

I am told that some years after Sir Wilfred T. Grenfell, the medical missionary to Labrador, had found Christ under the dynamic preaching of Dwight L. Moody, he met the American evangelist and said, "I want to thank you for leading me to Christ." Moody asked bluntly, "What have you been doing since?" "Helping others to know Christ," Grenfell replied. "Do you have any regrets?" To which the great missionary responded, "My only regret is for those who must hang their heads in shame when asked what have they been doing since they accepted Christ as Savior."

Those who are consecrated to the Lord's work are members of a great and glorious fellowship that girdles the globe. Like concentric circles the influence of believers in local churches reaches to every shore and peoples.

> Elect from every nation,
>   Yet one o'er all the earth,
> Her charter of salvation
>   One Lord, one faith, one birth;
> One holy name she blesses,
>   Partakes one holy food,
> And to one hope she presses,
>   With every grace endued.[4]

When I think of the world-wide fellowship of believers, I am mindful of those who even in our generation have been "faithful unto death" and who most surely will receive "a crown of life" (Rev. 2:10). And I remember other servants of Christ in lands where persecution and trial make difficult a public witness. And others who live in lands which have achieved a new freedom and where Christian leadership is imperative if freedom and brotherhood are to flourish and endure. Among these is my friend, Dr. Tanimola Ayorinde, for some time pastor of the First Baptist Church in Lagos, Nigeria, and chairman of the board of the Nigerian Broadcasting Corporation. He came from a pagan background, was won to Christ by a missionary supported by a member of my Richmond church, and has become a leading and responsible citizen and consecrated Christian. His mother gave him a name having almost prophetic meaning, WHO KNOWS WHAT THIS BOY MAY BECOME. It is through consecrated men like him that the Kingdom grows and advances.

Fourthly, to be faithful with life you must *discipline your life*. Paul understood the necessity of this. Writing to those Corinthians who were playing fast and loose with elemental Christian truths, he said, "I keep under my body, and bring it into subjection" (1 Cor. 9:27) or "I bruise my own body and make it know its master" (NEB)—the language is that of an athletic competitor. Elsewhere an athletic figure of speech is employed with effectiveness: "Let us lay aside every weight, and the sin which doth so easily beset us, and let us run with patience the race that is set before us" (Heb. 12:1).

How tragic are those well-meaning persons who, for the lack of self-discipline, fall short of the goal, go to pieces under the stress of temptation, and so fail to measure up to the high standards of Christian living. The temptations and trials of our day require disciplined and dedicated lives that God can use.

St. Francis of Assisi is said to have told a young friar, "There is no use going anywhere to preach, unless you preach everywhere you go." And the venerated friar practiced what he taught! A pious legend says that when he went with an invading army into Egypt, he constantly bore witness to his Savior. Many people thought he was a fanatic, but they goodnaturedly tolerated him. On one occasion he bore his witness to the Moslem king, who was deeply impressed with his sincerity and humility. Later when the invaders sued for peace and the opportunity to return to their homes, the king said, "I am letting you go free for the sake of the one man among you whose faith is not belied by his deeds." The faithful witness of a disciplined life has ever and again opened the doors of new life for others.

God grant that nothing in our life and witness will become a stumbling block in the path of any man who seeks Christ. How wonderful it would be if others could say of us what Henry M. Stanley is reported to have said of David Livingstone: "When I saw his patience, his unswerving zeal, and the changed lives of the Africans about him, I became a Christian without his ever saying a word to me about it."

Fifthly, to be faithful with life you must *expend your life*. Is not this what the Savior meant when he said, "Greater love hath no man than this, that a man lay down his life for his friends" (John 15:13)? "Expendable" is a word from the vocabulary of wartime. In the hands of a military commander anything, whether men, machines, or matériel, is expendable if essential to gain or hold an objective. The willingness to be expendable was expressed by my friend, Theron Rankin, a beloved missionary, who, facing the coming of war in China, said, "It may be that some of us must die for Christ in this generation." Certainly that represents the mind of Christ. His detractors said of him, "He saved others; himself he cannot save" (Mark 15:31).

When in our church the people were singing an invitation hymn, "I Surrender All," a young Christian came forward to dedicate his life to fulltime Christian service. I asked him to express his dedication in his own words, and he said in moving simplicity, "I surrender all." J. Lewis Schuck placed a slip of paper on which was written, "I give myself," in the collection plate at a missionary meeting, and thereupon embarked on a pioneer missionary career.

We too have been called to expend ourselves and to go into all the world with a gospel for all of life. Our day requires that we

> not only send missionaries but also live with a sense of mission;
>
> not only pass resolutions but also bring to pass a Christian revolution;
>
> not only speak words but also perform deeds;
>
> not only make a profession of our faith but also practice it in daily life and apply the abiding truth of Christ to the times in which we live.

We must match our lives against the life of our day and Christ's truths with the tension and turmoil of our generation. We must do battle with such age-old problems as the curse of liquor and corrupting immorality. As never before we face the mounting stress caused by racial discrimination and injustice. No wonder that some men doubt that the dream of peace on earth, good will toward men will ever become a reality.

Is it not imperative that in a time of world-wide confusion our churches become channels of healing love and understanding? We seek not just to maintain the status quo or to offer superficial answers to pressing problems and concerns, but to demonstrate and foster genuine good will, brotherhood, and peace according to the principles and spirit of our living Lord.

We need to pray as did my brother Earl for "the world that is not yet but ought to be." This is the prayer he wrote shortly before the end of an all too brief life gladly expended for Christ and his Kingdom:

> Bless, O Lord, our great nation and grant that we may ever share in the fulfillment of the prayer of the ancient prophet that "justice may roll down as waters and righteousness as a mighty stream."

Correct us, O Lord, where we are wrong. Confirm us wherever we may be right. Grant us wisdom to distinguish thy will and courage to do it. Give to each of us a steadfast heart which no unworthy affection may drag down, a clear vision which cannot be warped away from truth, and a firm loyalty which cannot be tempted aside.

As we have mastered nature, so that we might gain wealth, help us now to master the social relations of mankind that we may gain justice, peace, and a spirit of brotherhood.

Remind us that only the humble may house thee, only the pure in heart may see thee, only the merciful may know thee, only the brave may experience thee, and only the patient may serve thee truly.

Grant us a vision of the world that is not yet but ought to be, and in loyal devotion to its appearing grant us the peace of those who strive for it in spirit and in truth. Amen.

Only as we expend our lives, choosing to use them and lose them for Christ's sake, shall we know the joy that filled and overflowed from his heart. How strange to our secular ears and yet how spiritually meaningful are the words, "For the joy that was set before him [Jesus] endured the cross, despising the shame" (Heb. 12:2). He offers to us his joy, and it shall indeed be ours if we take up our crosses and follow him.

A preacher complained to Dr. E. Stanley Jones, saying, "My members are crucifying me." Dr. Jones gave him a challenging reply, "Our Lord didn't come down from his cross," and the preacher returned to his parish with a new spirit and devotion. During the following year he was instrumental in winning more than two hundred persons to Christ!

Sixthly, to be faithful with life—to use it and lose it for Christ and his Kingdom—is to *find your life*. Did the Apostle Paul, who urged the Corinthians to be faithful stewards, attempt to save his life and to avoid "the slings and arrows of outrageous fortune"?[5] No, he gave himself without equivocation to the ministry to which Christ called him. Here is his recital of the high cost of his discipleship:

> Of the Jews five times received I forty
> stripes save one.
> Thrice was I beaten with rods,
> one was I stoned,
> thrice I suffered shipwreck . . .
> In journeyings often,
> in perils of waters,

in perils of robbers,
in perils of mine own countrymen,
in perils by the heathen,
in perils in the city,
in perils in the wilderness,
in perils in the sea,
in perils among false brethren;
in weariness and painfulness,
in watchings often,
in hunger and thirst,
in fasting often,
in cold and nakedness.

2 Cor. 11:24-27

But did he, in losing life, find it? Listen to his answer: "I am crucified with Christ: nevertheless I live; yet not I, but Christ liveth in me: and the life which I now live in the flesh I live by the faith of the Son of God, who loved me, and gave himself for me" (Gal. 2:20). And once more resorting to the figurative language of athletics, Paul speaks in radiant and victorious words, "I have fought a good fight, I have finished my course, I have kept the faith: henceforth there is laid up for me a crown of righteousness" (2 Tim. 4:7-8).

What may the faithful further claim? Christ's assurance that "I go to prepare a place for you. And if I go and prepare a place for you, I will come again, and receive you unto myself" (John 14:2-3).

Life eternal is not a promise that is fulfilled only in the next world. We know it now in the inner joy and peace that the living Christ gives. And we shall be more faithful with life here and now when the eternal perspective voiced by a young missionary to China becomes our own prayer:

Lord, send me anywhere, only go with me;
Put any burden on me, only sustain me;
Sever any earthly tie save that which
    binds my heart to Thee.

If we are to be found faithful with the one life we are given, we must accept it as a gift from God, better it with the divine aid that is so freely available to us, consecrate it to the service of God, discipline it by the power of God, expend it to the glory of God—and we shall find it again for time and eternity by the grace of God in Christ

Jesus. The confident expectation of those who are faithful with life is expressed in these meaningful stanzas:

> God of grace and God of glory,
> On Thy people pour Thy power;
> Crown Thine ancient church's story;
> Bring her bud to glorious flower.
> Grant us wisdom, grant us courage,
> For the facing of this hour.
>
> Lo! the hosts of evil round us
> Scorn Thy Christ, assail his ways!
> From the fears that long have bound us
> Free our hearts to faith and praise.
> Grant us wisdom, grant us courage,
> For the living of these days.
>
> *
>
> Set our feet on lofty places;
> Gird our lives that they may be
> Armored with all Christ-like graces
> In the fight to set men free.
> Grant us wisdom, grant us courage,
> That we fail not man nor Thee![6]

The huge statue of Christ the Lord on Corcovado towers over Rio de Janeiro in blessing and benediction. Yet as one turns from that majestic figure to the unheeding people in the streets, he can only plead:

> O Master, from the mountain side,
> Make haste to heal these hearts of pain;
> Among these restless throngs abide,
> O tread the city's streets again.

God grant that though the figure remains upon the height, the living Christ may walk our streets in spirit and in truth and in the hearts of those who are faithful in their stewardship with life.

> Till sons of men shall learn Thy love
> And follow where Thy feet have trod;
> Till, glorious from Thy heaven above,
> Shall come the City of our God![7]

12.

How to Live in Peace

THE ANCIENT WORDS OF the prophet, "They shall beat their swords into plowshares, and their spears into pruninghooks: nation shall not lift up sword against nation, neither shall they learn war any more" (Isa. 2:4), have inspired and challenged mankind for centuries. Today, perhaps more than in any preceding generation, the aspiration for peace represents the universal desire and anxious longing of all men.

It is a sorry commentary on human nature that in a day when peace is so urgently required, some fanatical men jeopardize our tenuous peace by their mad pursuit of power, possessions, and prestige. Even more tragic is the fact that, although our technological genius has almost made the world a neighborhood, we have failed to learn how to live as good neighbors.

During a Middle Eastern crisis an Iranian, who was a fellow passenger with an American in a taxicab, translated a brief news broadcast and then added disconsolately, "God must be very sad today. He wants us to love each other and to live as brothers." Indeed he does! He sent his Son to earth to proclaim peace on earth and good will among men. The Apostle Paul wrote that Christ "is our peace" (Eph. 2:14).

Although the dawn of a genuine international peace seems at times to elude our fondest hopes and earnest efforts, it is possible to achieve peace within ourselves and to live at peace with others.

Two artists, each attempting to portray on canvas the concept of peace, produced widely divergent results. In the one a beautiful lake, upon which shadows stretch like the long, slim fingers of a musician, is portrayed between a fold of hills. A truly peaceful scene! The other depicts a devastating storm before which great trees bend limply. At the center of the canvas is a tiny bird, secure and at rest within a cleft in a rock. Peace amid turmoil and tension! If we are to find peace in our chaotic generation, it must be of the latter kind.

> At the heart of the cyclone tearing the sky
> And flinging the clouds and the towers by,
>   Is a place of central calm:
> So here in the roar of mortal things,
> I have a place where my spirit sings,
>   In the hollow of God's Palm.[1]

I

How may we find peace within the context of our daily lives? Here are two suggestions. First, we must make our peace with God. Jesus is the Prince of Peace. He came not only to rule the hearts of men and bring peace between nations—and he has been the greatest power for reconciliation the world has known—but also to show us the way to make our personal peace with God. Through faith in Christ we find forgiveness for our sin, release from the binding chains of guilt and fear, and a new sense of oneness with our heavenly Father. "At that time ye were without Christ, being aliens from the commonwealth of Israel, and strangers from the covenants of promise, having no hope, and without God in the world: but now in Christ Jesus ye who sometimes were far off are made nigh by the blood of Christ" (Eph. 2:12-13). A page from an ancient and dusty parchment only? Ah, no! A page which records our present-day predicament and affirms our hope.

A candidate for foreign mission service recalls that as a little lad he heard a preacher describe how awful it is to be lost. The boy felt miserably and hopelessly lost, and he did not know how to be found.

When the minister gave an invitation for Christian decision, the boy, quivering and shaking, went forward. Because he was such a little lad and had slipped into a seat next to the stove at the front of the small church, the preacher, if he noticed at all, presumed that the boy was cold. Later the lad talked with his pastor and parents and came to know what it means to accept Jesus as Savior. Now a laborer in God's vineyard, he says, "Ever since I made that decision I have had such inner peace and joy that I want to share it with others across the broad seas." This inner peace is God's gift to all who receive the Lord Christ as Savior and seek to serve him.

Secondly, if we wish to find peace, we must learn to make peace with others. It is not always easy to confess our sins and to ask for forgiveness, but harmony and reconciliation lie along this pathway. Nor is it usually easy for us to forgive those who have wronged us, but we must forgive others their trespasses if we would claim God's forgiveness for our sins. "As much as lieth in you," counseled the Apostle Paul, "live peaceably with all men" (Rom. 12:18).

Here is a letter from a young woman who formerly worshiped in the church I serve. It speaks for itself and offers its own testimony.

Now after many years I want to express my thanks for a sermon you preached. You must surely have forgotten the sermon, and I would never have thought that after so long a time it would have offered me such a healing word.

To say that my next-door neighbor and I were not on speaking terms is a mild statement of the facts. I was very angry with her and she with me. We even prohibited our children from playing with each other. The tension across our fence was almost electric!

One day my nerves were at the breaking point. I had to do something. Then I remembered a sermon of yours on our need to forgive other people. Every word seemed to come back sharply and clearly.

So I baked a cake and walked almost apprehensively to my neighbor's door. I wasn't sure how I would be received. But I held out the cake and said, "Please accept this as a gift of love and forgive me." My neighbor opened wide her arms and asked for my forgiveness too.

Now there is peace in our neighborhood and peace and joy in my heart.

How can we conceivably have peace among nations if we do not first have peace among neighbors? True peace must begin at home. We need, therefore, to cultivate those inner attitudes that make for peace with God and with others.

II

An important first step toward spiritual peace is *self-discipline.* We need to control ourselves and avoid those excesses for which we must later offer apologies. We need such discipline so that we do not behave in childish ways, but rather act in a manner that is becoming to mature persons. "He that is slow to anger is better than the mighty; and he that ruleth his spirit than he that taketh a city" (Prov. 16:32). We shall master ourselves when we are mastered in turn by Christ our Lord and seek to live in his spirit and by his principles.

Self-acceptance is also prerequisite to the achievement of inner peace. We need to learn to accept ourselves as we are. Rose-tinted glasses turned on ourselves will not do. We must come to terms with our limitations and handicaps—and each of us has them—and then resolve with God's gracious help to be the best possible persons despite circumstances over which we may have little real control. Some conditions can never be changed, but we can live joyfully and usefully in spite of them. We need not look far to discover that joy and peace are not found only in healthy bodies or wealthy homes. The manger of Bethlehem cradled a King. The Apostle Paul persisted in giving a radiant Christian witness though he was plagued by his thorn in the flesh. Often in humble hearts and simple homes may be found glowing lives after people have learned to accept with equanimity what life has brought.

An additional discipline essential for peace with others is *self-giving.* The real joy of living is in giving. As we give ourselves in love and concern to others, both we and they find the deeper meanings of life. The beautiful play, *The Sound of Music,* portrays the trials of the Trapp family when they were compelled to flee as refugees from their homeland. Their escape was made possible by a young man who, though deeply in love with a girl in the Trapp family, remained behind so that his beloved might find freedom. The mother of the family articulates the spirit of self-giving in a single priceless sentence: "Love isn't really love till you give it away."

Self-acceptance, self-giving, and self-discipline are keys which will unlock even the most distrustful and obdurate hearts and permit the warm light of peace to enter. They bring healing to our own hearts so that we may help to heal differences between men. In A. J. Cronin's novel, *The Keys of the Kingdom,* Mr. Chia speaks to Father Chisholm in these moving words:

> My friend, I have often said: There are many religions and each has its gate to heaven. . . . Now it would appear that I have the extraordinary desire to enter by your gate. . . Once, many years ago, when you cured my son, I was not serious. But then I was unaware of the nature of your life. . . of its patience, quietness and courage. The goodness of a religion is best judged by the goodness of its adherents. My friend . . . you have conquered me by example.[2]

Here indeed is seen the rich harvest that follows acceptance, discipline, and giving!

III

In a similar spirit we must dedicate ourselves to great and worthy endeavors. True peace is not complacency or a lack of concern. True peace comes when we feel assured that we are where God wants us to be and are doing what he has called us to do. Through service in your church and community as well as in the larger work of the Kingdom of God, all men, even the humblest and least talented, may find satisfaction and a sense of meaningful achievement.

A young man, about to embark with his family to the mission field, told of the struggle which preceded his decision to be a missionary. He was miserably unhappy in his pastorate and he had no peace of mind, for he was convinced that God had chosen one field of work for him and he had chosen another. At home one morning he hurried to help his daughter who was crying as though her heart would break. Pointing to a little fish that had jumped out of the aquarium and was dying on the floor, the child exclaimed, "Daddy, he is where he doesn't belong, isn't he?"

That did it! The father saw in the fish's predicament and his daughter's words the position in which he found himself. Then and there, he determined to go where he knew God was leading him.

Now on the threshold of a new spiritual adventure, he said, "I have peace in my heart tonight because I am going to be where God wants me to be, and I shall be doing what God wants me to do."

Peace is a gift God offers to all who will accept it and share it. Long ago the angels of the Nativity sang, "Glory to God in the highest, and on earth peace, good will toward men" (Luke 2:14). Come what may, a Christian can be ready and sufficient for any test. He will know peace and poise in his own heart and good will toward all men, if he gives God priority in his life and permits the love of God to shine in his heart and through his life.

A pastor in a Southern community put this truth to a real test. He had been a well-known basketball player. After the broadcast of a game in which he had participated, he received a letter from a convict in a state penitentiary. They corresponded for several years. When finally the convict was released on parole, the minister invited him to come to his own home for Christmas.

On Christmas morning when gifts were distributed by the minister, his wife, and children, each had wrapped something for their guest. After a time the parolee slipped quietly from the room. When the minister found him later, the guest had tears in his eyes. "So much love," he said, "and I am so unworthy."

That Christmas, within a home circle of those who loved the Lord, he found a new life of peace and joy in Christ. To this day he is a disciple of him who said, "Peace I leave with you, my peace I give unto you: not as the world giveth, give I unto you. Let not your heart be troubled" (John 14:27).

This peace of God can be yours as you learn to know and trust him as the Father who was so real to Jesus. It will sustain you both in the tensions of daily life and the crises that come to us all. Such is the witness of a young woman who had to face a crushing sorrow, but did it with a radiant faith that blessed and inspired others. Her secret is revealed in a letter to her pastor:

"I realize God is such a great comfort to one at this time or any time, and I am so glad I know him."

With such a personal faith, "The Peace of God, which passeth all understanding, shall keep your hearts and minds through Christ Jesus" (Phil. 4:7).

13.

How the Lord Helps Those
Who Help Themselves

A MINISTER RECEIVES TELEPHONE calls on almost every conceivable subject. Hardly a week passes during which I am not asked to settle by phone some argument about religion, church practice, or a Scripture verse. Often callers ask, "Preacher, where can I find such and such in the Bible?" I keep a concordance handy both at home and in my church study because questioners frequently mention verses which are altogether new to me; often I find these are not in the Bible.

A "verse" I have been asked on more than one occasion to identify by chapter and verse is "The Lord helps those who help themselves." If you spend a week of Sundays and read the Bible from Genesis to Revelation, you will not find that verse. But many people think it is there, and some will even argue that they remember having seen it in the Bible. This proverb, however, may be found in a number of non-biblical sources, and there are numerous variations such as "To complete the design of the gods we have to put a stitch here and there,"[1] or "The whole trouble is that we won't let God help us,"[2] or " 'Let God do it all,' someone will say; but if man folds his arms, God will go to sleep."[3]

I might suggest to my questioners two verses which I can guarantee *are* in the Bible—"We are labourers together with God" (1 Cor. 3:9) and "My help cometh from the Lord" (Ps. 121:2)—but they would say, "No, no, they're not what I have in mind." A verse which somewhat approximates the proverb is the one which Captain John Smith used so effectively in the early months at Jamestown: "If any would not work, neither should he eat" (2 Thess. 3:10).

Although not found in the Bible, the words "The Lord helps those who help themselves" do contain a measure of truth. Yet it is susceptible to much misinterpretation. People employ this old saying to justify selfish actions. They argue, "If I don't look out for number one, nobody is going to. The Lord helps those who help themselves, you know." Seeking to profit at another person's expense, they try to vindicate their behavior by quoting from the Bible. At such times I am glad the proverb is not in the Bible. Yet there is real truth in the thought that the Lord helps those who help themselves.

This is undergirded by the prophet Isaiah: "They that wait upon the Lord shall renew their strength; they shall mount up with wings as eagles; they shall run, and not be weary; and they shall walk, and not faint" (Isa. 40:31). Why? The renewing of their strength comes from God. And again the prophet says, "I the Lord thy God will hold thy right hand, saying unto thee, Fear not; I will help thee" (Isa. 41:13). God promises to support those who are righteous.

Like an earthly father, God at times can help us only when we help ourselves. If we do what he expects of us, then he does his part. This is something each of us understands. A father, for instance, is most anxious that his son acquire the benefits of a college education. Knowing how important a sound education is, the father submits an application to the university, sees that his son is properly enrolled, and pays the bills. But at college the boy becomes involved in a multitude of outside activities and the lessons are neglected. At the end of the first semester the son flunks out. However much the father wants his son to have an education, he cannot give it to him. A college degree is something a young man must earn for himself. If he does not do his part, all the money in the world cannot secure an education for him. In a similar fashion the Lord helps those who help themselves. Time and again that is the only way he can help.

After generations of bitter slavery in Egypt, the Lord opened the way for the children of Israel to leave. But he could not push them; they had to be willing to leave their homes and all they had acquired during the period of bondage and travel into an unknown wilderness. When food was scarce during their sojourn, many bemoaned the loss of the fleshpots of Egypt. When hardships and difficulties marked their slow progress, many complained to Moses and asked why he had led them into the desert to die. God could reward their efforts with freedom only after they had made a resolute and determined advance into Canaan.

Another qualification must be considered when we say that the Lord helps those who help themselves. God's help is contingent upon our choice of worthy ends, means that are in keeping with his spirit, and objectives that are consistent with his will. God will never stoop to anything that is low and unworthy merely because we happen to want it. We could never expect the God and Father of all mankind to help us at the expense of another person whom he loves as much as he loves us.

Otherwise, if we assume the proper initiative, we have his assurance of guidance and support. A dedicated man and the power of the Almighty joining forces produce an unbeatable combination. Here are some of the ways in which this is true.

I

God helps those who cannot help themselves. A man having only one leg and supporting himself on crutches makes his way slowly to a sacred shrine. A passerby watches and asks a companion, "Do you think that fellow believes the Lord will give him another leg if he prays hard enough?" Overhearing the comment, the cripple says, "I don't expect the Lord to give me another leg, but I do expect him to answer my prayer to help me to make the best use of the one I have."

At one time or another each of us is in the position of not being able to do anything about a particular situation or condition. Having exhausted all human resources, we have no alternative other than to admit, "There is nothing more I can do. It is now in the hands of the Lord." Our mistake often is that we do not turn to him until we have reached the end of our tether, but even then his love is unfailing. When we can no longer help ourselves, we are not without help.

A World War II bomber pilot was an orphan, left largely to manage for himself. In his youth he sought for a philosophy of life that would justify his standing on his own feet, beholden to no one. Then in one air strike after another over Berlin he realized how helpless he really was. He flew a plane, but he did not even carry a gun. The circumstances in which he found himself seemed utterly beyond his control. But as he thought about the helplessness of man, he recalled long-forgotten words: "When thou passest through the waters, I will be with thee; and through the rivers, they shall not overflow thee" (Isa. 43:2).

How helpless we are in all of the great crises of life! We are unable to say when we should be born or where or to whom. After birth we breathe, eat, and cry, but we are completely dependent on others for nourishment and care. Throughout childhood our lives are made or marred by parents, teachers, and friends who teach us love or hate, security or fear. In our later years sickness and accidents for which we may not even be responsible require the care and assistance of others.

And often we travel down dead-end streets. Sailing through the fjords of Norway, we moved through narrow strips of water between high rocky cliffs. Sometimes I wondered if the navigator really knew where he was going. But suddenly the ship would make a turn and around a bend would lie miles of water stretching ahead of us. What had seemed to be a dead-end was in fact an open gateway. How often it is true that we

> By faith, and faith alone, embrace,
> Believing where we cannot prove,

for

> We have but faith: we cannot know,
> For knowledge is of things we see;
> And yet we trust it comes from thee,
> A beam in darkness: let it grow.[4]

All men at times are so perplexed by the unknown that lies ahead of them that they fall to their knees and pray:

> Lead, kindly Light, amid the encircling gloom
> Lead thou me on!
> The night is dark, and I am far from home;
> Lead thou me on![5]

So we move on, knowing that when God closes one door he always opens another. And we confidently trust that at the end of life's pilgrimage there will be a golden casement opening to eternity. Jesus said—and we trust him in life and death—"I go to prepare a place for you" (John 14:2).

Of course, we have a responsibility in preparing ourselves for that journey across the Jordan, but our hope rests, not in our own sufficiency, but in God.

The Psalmist wrote, "Though the Lord be high, yet hath he respect unto the lowly. . . . Though I walk in the midst of trouble, thou wilt revive me: thou shalt stretch forth thine hand . . . and thy right hand shall save me" (Ps. 138:6-7). The Lord helps those who cannot help themselves. He is "not far from every one of us" (Acts 17:27). His love embraces us as does the sea the land. The clergyman in *The Lovely Ambition* by Mary Ellen Chase says thoughtfully:

> "Grace? Well, that's very difficult to explain, Mrs. Gowan. Many learned men have thought about grace for many centuries. Most of them think it has to do with forgiveness and mercy, but I'm inclined to disagree with them. I rather think grace means just the constant presence of God."[6]

Actually grace means that God treats us not as we deserve, but as we need. Ask those who are helpless to help themselves and they will tell you the deepest meaning of the words, "My grace is sufficient for thee: for my strength is made perfect in weakness" (2 Cor. 12:9).

II

God also helps those who help each other. We come closest to the spirit of the Lord Christ when we give a cup of cold water to a man in need. "Every one that loveth is born of God" (1 John 4:7). Indeed, "if God so loved us, we ought also to love one another" (1 John 4:11). Love for God and a corresponding love of man are inseparable components in our discipleship. *"Let me forget me,"* one of Graham Greene's characters prays. "Dear God, I've tried to love and I've made such a hash of it. If I could love You, I'd know how to love them."[7] That's the clue!

We must learn—and this is a difficult lesson—to put up with each other's faults and to forgive and forget. Forgetting is often more of a stumblingblock in human relationships than forgiving. But to heal broken bonds and then to help others and to serve worthy ends will bring God's blessing to us.

In the midst of one of his most impassioned passages on the glory and majesty of God and man's dependence upon him, Isaiah pauses for a moment to comment on another topic in which he says, "They helped every one his neighbour; and every one said to his brother, Be of good courage" (Isa. 41:6). The carpenter helped the gold-smith, and the goldsmith, the blacksmith. Could you find a more whole-some text? One thing only blights the beauty of these words: everyone in this instance was helping his neighbor in the making of idols!

It is good for men to work together, and Isaiah does not deride helping one's neighbor; but he points to the sin of co-operating to achieve an unworthy purpose. Even though every man helped his neighbor, you may be certain that no blessing crowned their endeavor.

But the Lord did promise divine aid to young Solomon after he had committed himself to serving his fellow men. After having been established on the throne of his father David, Solomon went to Gibeon to pray. God inquired of him saying, "Ask what I shall give thee." Solomon replied, "Give therefore thy servant an understanding heart to judge thy people, that I may discern between good and bad." So delighted was God that Solomon should place the welfare of his people above all else that he responded: "Because thou hast asked this thing, and hast not asked for thyself long life; neither hast asked riches for thyself, nor hast asked the life of thine enemies; but hast asked for thyself understanding to discern judgment; behold, I have done ac-cording to thy words: lo, I have given thee a wise and an under-standing heart. . . . And I have also given thee that which thou hast not asked, both riches and honour" (1 Kings 3:5, 9, 11-13).

When she received the British crown in Westminster Abbey, Elizabeth II vowed:

I declare before you all that my whole life, whether it be long or short, shall be devoted to your service and in the service of the great imperial family to which we all belong. But I shall not have the strength to carry out this resolution unless you join in it with me as I invite you now to do. I know that your support will be unfailing. God help me to make good my vow and God bless all of you who are willing to share it.

It is in this spirit that Christians are to help everyone his neighbor, and the Lord will surely help those who seek to help others in his name.

III

Furthermore, *God helps those who help him* and find their deepest joy in saying:

> Take my life, and let it be
> Consecrated, Lord, to Thee.[8]

Did not the Psalmist affirm this when he said, "The Lord God is a sun and shield: the Lord will give grace and glory: no good thing will he withhold from them that walk uprightly"? No good thing does he withhold from those who

> walk in his truth,
> stand for the right,
> oppose the powers of evil, and
> abide in his love.

We learn how true this is when we call the roll of Christian martyrs, missionaries, and dedicated laymen. They never felt that the Lord failed them. When the annual supply ship came too late, one missionary hero was found dead on the seashore. The last entry in his diary read, "I am overwhelmed by the goodness of God." Men had failed him, but God had not.

A friend, whose name I shall withhold lest he and his loved ones be jeopardized, has time and again risked his life and liberty to take the necessities of life to those who live on the other side of the Iron Curtain. He does not think of himself as a martyr nor claim a hero's crown, but he is doing his very best to strengthen the faith and meet the needs of those who live in an ungodly land.

God's support of those who engage in his work and ministry is unfailing. On this fact we can base our lives. This assurance is a guiding light by which we may confidently steer our course in life. But can the Lord depend as surely on us? Are we keeping faith with him? Do we, who so desperately need his help, seek ways in which we can help him?

One of the leaders of the Lutheran Church in divided Germany says about the tragic years when he was imprisoned for his faith:

As the hell within got worse, within the walls we were sustained by the constant assurance of the prayers of intercession for us offered by those outside the walls.

Christians around the world kept strong through prayer the never-failing tie of Christian love. God was faithful and a great witness thrilled the world. How often though some person falters, some work is left undone, or some cause fails because we have not done our part through prayer.

So great was the ministry of Charles H. Spurgeon, nineteenth-century London preacher, that a six-thousand-seat tabernacle was built so that his sermons might be heard by more people. When a reporter asked him for an explanation of his pulpit power, Spurgeon, without a moment's reflection, answered, "My people pray for me." How blessed are pastor and people who trust in God!

We may well refrain from using too freely the words, "The Lord helps those who help themselves," lest we think too much of personal benefit and reward. Yet the testimony of our Christian faith confirms the fact that God continually helps those who cannot help themselves, who devote their energies to helping others, and who dedicate themselves to helping him in the work of his Kingdom.

14.

How Prayer Can Mean More to You

WHEN A LITTLE GIRL was told that she was about to have an operation, she was understandably anxious. The doctor said, "Now you needn't worry. I am only going to put you to sleep for a little while." "Oh, if I am going to sleep," the girl said, "then I should say my prayers." As she was taken into the operating room, she closed her eyes and prayed, "Dear God, I don't know all these people, but you do. Bless the doctors and the nurses and mommie and daddy and me. Keep us all in thy love. Amen." Then after opening her eyes, she said, "All right, I am ready now."

With a disarming simplicity she expressed some of the meanings of prayer which erudite theologians talk about with big words and deep-browed disputation. Let us turn from erudition and argument and think about prayer with a childlike simplicity.

I

C. S. Lewis, an Oxford scholar, says that prayer is conversation and fellowship with God our Father. However else prayer may be described or defined, it is certainly that. "He that cometh to God must believe that he is, and that he is a rewarder of them that diligently seek him" (Heb. 11:6). Even a small child would nod in agreement if I were to say that there is a God and that we are privileged to communicate with him in prayer, confident that he will bless us according to our need.

In a somewhat different manner the prophet Micah wrote, "What doth the Lord require of thee, but to do justly, and to love mercy, and to walk humbly with thy God?" (Mic. 6:8). I like the simple language of Dr. Moffatt's translation, "What does the Eternal ask from you but to be just and kind and live in quiet fellowship with your God?" We have achieved a fundamental understanding of what prayer is when we think of it as fellowship with God. This brings a good deal more meaning into prayer than merely to regard it as asking God for something we need or crying out to him in a crisis.

Fellowship embraces many experiences. First, it means *talking with God*. We talk with One whom we know and love and who knows and cares for us. We do not have to bombard the cold walls of heaven with our pleas or beat down the door to be heard by him. When we talk with God, we are already assured of his love, his good will, his presence, and his deep concern for us.

I do not mean that we talk to God, but rather with him. "And the Lord spake unto Moses face to face, as a man speaketh unto his friend" (Exod. 33:11). Paul wrote to the Ephesians, "Now therefore ye are no more strangers and foreigners, but fellow-citizens with the saints, and of the household of God" (Eph. 2:19). Even as within a home a child talks face to face with his parents, so may we turn to God. The language of our homes is also the language of heaven: "I love you," "I trust you," "I need you," "I am sorry," "Please help me," "I don't quite understand," and "What can I do for you?"

Secondly, prayer is not only talking but also *listening to God*. A little girl knelt at her bedside for a prolonged period. Finally her mother said, "Get up now and go to bed." To which the youngster replied, "Well, I have finished talking to God, but I'm waiting to see what he has to say to me." We need to wait for God's voice and to sense his nearness to us. "Enoch walked with God" (Gen. 5:22). He knew the meaning of the divine comradeship that listening to God makes possible. Abraham heard God say go, and "he went out, not knowing whither he went. . . . For he looked for a city which hath foundations, whose builder and maker is God" (Heb. 11:8, 10). When Moses listened for God's word of guidance, he became the deliverer of his people.

Thirdly, the fellowship of prayer includes *responding to God*. Our response is predicated upon God's concern for us. "Ye shall seek me, and find me, when ye shall search for me with all your heart" (Jer. 29:13). The initiative is God's, and our response is based on his assurance and promise.

What must be the character of our response? We are instructed to love the Lord with our whole beings. We must not neglect our wills.

> Our wills are ours, we know not how;
> Our wills are ours, to make them thine.[1]

Nor our minds. "O God," exclaimed the astronomer Kepler, "I am thinking Thy thoughts after Thee."[2] Nor our feelings of love, guilt, insecurity, and loneliness. As the Children of Israel move past him and into the Promised Land, Moses in the folk drama *The Green Pastures* turns to God, saying, "Yere I is, Lawd. De chillun is goin' into de Promised Land. You's with me, ain't you, Lawd?" God places his hands on the shoulders of the aging leader and replies, "Co'se I is."[3]

Our only worthy response to God's initiative and concern is expressed in the familiar words:

> Take my heart, it is Thine own;
> It shall be Thy royal throne.[4]

II

"Prayer," wrote Martin Luther, "is a strong wall and fortress of the church; it is a goodly Christian's weapon."[5] And so it is. We need to know how prayer may mean more to us, for prayer is the lifeblood of Christian devotion.

Here, as in so many other circumstances, Jesus is our example. His life was centered in prayer. He turned to his Father before every personal crisis and decision. So close was their communion that Jesus could say, "I and my Father are one" (John 10:30).

He prayed when tempted in the wilderness.

His choice of his disciples was preceded by prayer.

Rising before daybreak, he leaned his arms upon the windowsill of heaven and found strength for the hours which were to follow.

He prayed during his agonizing watch in Gethsemane.

At life's extremity, when his body had been lifted upon a cross, he relied again on this lifelong discipline.

Jesus knew the vital importance of prayer and that we cannot live spiritually without prayer any more readily than we can live physically without bread and water. In the far country the prodigal said, "I will arise and go to my father" (Luke 15:18). He found that his father still loved him and cared and understood. Within the enfolding arms of his father, he found new life. The prodigal knew where to go, and so do we.

It is strange, isn't it, that knowing this, we do not pray more regularly, more consistently, and more thoughtfully? We need to give more time to prayer. We need to

> Take time to be holy, speak oft with thy Lord;
> Abide in Him always, and feed on His Word.[6]

Jesus was never rushed. He seemed never to have been pushing the clock. He did nothing helter-skelter. Times of prayer were for him periods of refreshment and renewal.

Jesus also gave us an example regarding the importance of thinking of prayer as a wholesome, life-lifting experience. Through prayer he was always in tune with the Eternal. The importance of this came home to me one day when I was making pastoral calls in the country. Occasionally county numbers are confusing. After trying to follow landmarks and guideposts, I was about to throw up my hands in despair when along came a county policeman. He was no better off than I. In his hand he carried a summons, but he could not find the right number to serve it. But he had an answer to both of our problems. By merely pressing a button, he was able to talk with headquarters and we both were helped on our way. By praying we too may keep in touch with our spiritual Headquarters.

Jesus taught us more than this. He practiced personal prayer and common prayer. "Where two or there gathered together in my name, there am I in the midst of them" (Matt. 18:20). In his name we pray together each time we link our hearts in worship in the Lord's

House. Many of the hymns we sing are in fact prayers by which we give voice to our common petitions. Grace at meals and daily devotions at the family altar are prayer periods which Jesus commended and in which he shares our fellowship.

Many years ago in the mountains of New York State I dug a well. Down through rocky soil I went until I came to muddy water that I knew to be surface drainage. I had to go down deeper. At last I experienced the thrill of watching clean, fresh water gush from a spring beneath a large rock. For how long a time that water had been trying to reach the surface, I do not know. But after sinking tile and providing sand as a filter, I was able to claim sweet-tasting water. The water had always been there. All I needed to do was to tap it. By prayer we tap the unfailing resources of God.

III

Now the Bible makes it perfectly clear that some prayers are futile. We read, for instance, of the folly and futility of praying just to impress God. Jesus said, "When you pray don't rattle off long prayers like the pagans who think they will be heard because they use so many words" (Matt. 6:7, PHILLIPS). We do not need to impress God any more than we would need to curry the favor of a friend.

It is likewise futile to pray merely to be seen of men. Did Jesus ever speak more bitingly than when he described pompous people who pray in public places so they may win the plaudits of undiscerning people? Mark carefully the scorn found in his appraisal and judgment: "When you pray, don't be like the playactors. They love to stand in the synagogues and at street corners so that people may see them at it. Believe me, they have had all the reward they are going to get!" Rather he advised, "When you pray, go into your own room, shut your door and pray to your Father privately." (Matt. 6:5-6, PHILLIPS).

Futile also is prayer when we strive to inflate our own ego. Jesus told of a Pharisee who stood in the temple and "prayed thus with himself, God, I thank thee, that I am not as other men." He rehearsed his spiritual achievements and told God that he was so much better than other men. Jesus observed that the Pharisee's self-righteousness deprived him of justification. But the humble publican who stood within the shadows and prayed, "God be merciful to me a sinner," was justified. (Luke 18:10-14.)

And futile, too, are prayers we offer as though we had an Aladdin's lamp. If we rub hard enough, hocus-pocus, wonderful things will happen! But God's children need no magic tricks to win divine blessings. Far from it. There is mystery in prayer, to be sure.

> More things are wrought by prayer
> Than this world dreams of.[7]

But this is beyond the range of human prediction or understanding. Someone has commented, "You can ask anything of God, but you cannot demand anything." When we ask, we put our trust in God's love, wisdom, and concern; but when we demand, we wish to substitute our wisdom for that of the Almighty.

IV

How then shall we pray? Let us turn to the Lord's Prayer for an answer. This prayer teaches us to pray *unselfishly*. We begin by saying, not "My Father," but "Our Father." We cannot pray to our Father for that which concerns and benefits only us individually. Jesus wants us to claim for ourselves those things which we hope other men may share equally. He gives to us a sense of unity and oneness within the fellowship of praying hearts. In *The Big Fisherman* by Lloyd C. Douglas the Roman Mencius receives this message from his friend Voldi:

My own opinion of the mysterious Nazarene is difficult to define. On first sight of him I was a bit disappointed. He is not an heroic figure but the man has a compelling voice. I can't describe it or the effect of it. It's a unifying voice that converts a great crowd of mutually distrustful strangers into a tight little group of blood relatives.[8]

The Apostle Paul wrote, "There is one body, and one Spirit, even as ye are called in one hope of your calling" (Eph. 4:4). In his high priestly prayer, Jesus asked that "they may be one, as we are" (John 17:11). The Lord's Prayer begins where all true prayer begins—with the word "*our*."

This prayer also bids us to pray *reverently*. Impressed by the greatness and goodness, the majesty and glory of the Eternal, we lift our hearts to him and say, "Hallowed by thy name." This means "thy name be revered" (MOFFATT) and "may your name be honored" (PHILLIPS). God's name is sacred and is so held and honored by those who love him. "Holy, holy, holy, is the Lord of hosts: the whole earth is full of his glory" (Isa. 6:3).

To unselfishness and reverence is added *vision*. In prayer we reach beyond things as they are to a vision of a world wherein dwells righteousness, brotherhood, justice, and peace. "Thy kingdom come. Thy will be done, in earth, as it is in heaven."

> O Lord of life, Thy kingdom is at hand,
> Blest reign of love and liberty and light;
> Time long foretold by seers of every land;
> The cherished dream of watchers through
> the night.[9]

The Lord's Prayer also instructs us to pray *specifically*. Even while we contemplate the Kingdom which is to come, we turn unashamedly to petition God for such mundane necessities as our daily bread. The prodigality of God extends to our most minute physical craving and requirement. His sun and showers bring to fruition the golden shaft of wheat.

Our prayers for forgiveness have meaning only when we pray in a *forgiving spirit*. Anticipating God's generous forgiveness of our disobedience and sin just as generously we proffer forgiveness to those who have wronged us. Only in this way can we truly expect God to cleanse our evil lives and guard us against harsh judgments and ensnaring temptations. He forgives as we forgive.

Finally, the model prayer calls us to pray *faithfully*. The prayer which Jesus taught his disciples concludes with a radiant assurance of victory: "Thine is the kingdom, and the power, and the glory, for ever." By faith we know that one day we shall pass through those gates of splendor, and we shall be victors then as now and through endless days.

V

The Bible identifies many kinds of prayer. We do not ordinarily include every form in a single prayer, yet each is a facet in our prayer experience. Most commonly, prayer is *communion*. Through prayer we become aware of a living fellowship with God. He and we are at one.

One of the more frequently neglected forms of prayer is *adoration*. To look lovingly upon God for his own sake only and to feast our hearts in worship and devotion gives us a feeling of the greatness and completeness that belong to him alone. Isaiah knew the meaning and joy of adoration when he exclaimed, "I saw also the Lord sitting upon a throne, high and lifted up, and his train filled the temple" (Isa. 6:1).

The prayer of *thanksgiving* is a measure of our appreciation for all that God has done for us. Once yearly we observe Thanksgiving Day, and rightly so. Paul reminds us, however, that we are to give "thanks always for all things" (Eph. 5:20). "Some people," Elizabeth Barrett Browning wrote, "always sigh in thanking God."[10] Do we take too much for granted or do we somehow feel that we have the right to expect all of the evidences of divine beneficence? How much more appropriate it is to

> Count your many blessings, name them one by one,
> And it will surprise you what the Lord hath done.[11]

After thanksgiving should come the prayer of *confession*. Each of us has felt—or surely should have—as did the chastened prodigal who said, "I have sinned against heaven, and in thy sight, and am no more worthy to be called thy son" (Luke 15:21). God's forgiveness and blessing follows our penitence. Confession is prerequisite to healing and restoration. Even the great Isaiah knew this, and surely this helps to account for his towering spiritual grandeur. He said, "I am a man of unclean lips, and I dwell in the midst of a people of unclean lips" (Isa. 6:5). In vain do we ask, "Create in me a clean heart, O God; and renew a right spirit within me" (Ps. 51:10), unless we also acknowledge a sense of our sinfulness.

Intercession is a type of prayer which binds our sorrows and joys, our trials and aspirations, to the whole worshiping community. We pray for those who have not the wit or wisdom to pray for themselves. We pray for our brethren of every race and nation, knowing that as we lift our hands in their behalf they, too, are remembering us at the Throne of Grace.

> For so the whole round earth is every way
> Bound by gold chains about the feet of God.[12]

Was there ever a generation in which so many people needed our prayers? Archibald MacLeish portrays two circus roustabouts who show an uncanny perception of the dilemma men face. The one, Mr. Zuss, says:

> Oh, there's always
> Someone playing Job.

And his companion Nickles replies:

> There must be
> Thousands!
>
> *
>
> Millions and millions of mankind
> Burned, crushed, broken, mutilated,
> Slaughtered, and for what? For thinking!
> For walking round the world in the wrong
> Skin, the wrong-shaped noses, eyelids:
> Sleeping the wrong night in the wrong city—
> London, Dresden, Hiroshima.
> There never could have been so many
> Suffered more for less.[13]

Not only humanity but also individual persons are standing in the need of our prayers. A man who lives a thousand miles away wrote to me to express his thankfulness that my father had long ago prayed for him, visited in his home, and led him to accept Jesus Christ as his Savior.

I almost didn't accept Him, but your father read to me from Romans— "The wages of sin is death; but the gift of God is eternal life through Jesus Christ our Lord." When I heard those words I accepted God's gift.

Through the years he has lived a godly and useful life. But more than anything else he wrote, these words most touched me: "Ted, I want you to know that every day I pray for you and your ministry." I am blessed and humbled that a dear old man intercedes for me day after day as my father did for him years ago.

Surely we must pray for others, but we need also to pray for ourselves. Our personal needs often come into true perspective after we have prayed for other men. This brings us to the last element in prayer—*dedication.* Having prayed for courage, strength, guidance, and bread—or whatever our need may be—we should consecrate all that we have and are to God's purpose for our lives. Sometimes surrender should be our first petition; always no prayer is complete until we have said, "Thy will be done."

Charles Welborn tells of a young man who hesitated to give himself to Christ. Then Welborn said, "I am going to pray for you, and then you can pray for yourself." When it came time for the youth to pray, he said, "I don't know how to pray. The only prayer I know is the Lord's Prayer which I learned when I was a little boy." Welborn encouraged him, saying, "Then pray that prayer, but mean every word you pray." Slowly he began, "Our Father which art in heaven, Hallowed be thy name. Thy kingdom come. Thy will be done—thy will be done." Grasping the preacher by the hand, he said, "I want his will to be done in me." And a new life began for him as it can and indeed will for all those who truly pray.

15.

How the Bible Can Mean More to You

I HAVE BIBLES PUBLISHED in many languages, including Russian and English. Bibles are scarce in Russia. During a visit there I was told that people commonly borrow Bibles from friends and copy favorite verses in longhand so that they may have at least some of God's Word in their homes.

In our country, on the other hand, Bibles are available everywhere. You may secure them at corner drugstores or from airport vending machines. Isn't it ironical that in a nation where Bibles are printed in such large quantities so many people neglect their Bibles?

There are many reasons why we do not read the Bible as regularly as we should or as often as we know we ought. Sometimes our alibis are pretty flimsy, and sometimes our excuses indicate a misunderstanding of what the Bible is.

What is the Bible? Above all else, it is God's Word to us and not man's word, although it has been transmitted through men inspired by God and has been preserved, translated, and passed on to us by scholars who often risked their lives that we might have this precious Word for our day. For all Christians the Bible is inestimably valuable, for it tells the story of Jesus, the Word of God Incarnate, who is "the

Word . . . made flesh, and dwelt among us . . . full of grace and truth" (John 1:14).

What manifold treasures are hidden in this priceless spiritual ore! Here are revealed the truths of creation and of eternity, and a rich inspiration for all of the passing years. Yet we neglect this pearl of great price, or turn to its pages only for special occasions or on particular days.

When archaeologists were excavating at the site of the ancient city of Shechem, an old clay pot was uncovered. At first the pot did not seem to be a very promising relic, but when it was opened thirty-five valuable coins from an old dynasty were found within. Similar treasures await those who open their Bibles!

I

In the remarkable Psalm 119, which is not only the longest chapter in the Bible but also one of the most ingenious, are suggested some of the treasures to be found in God's Word, verse 9 promises cleansing: "Wherewithal shall a young man cleanse his way? by taking heed thereto according to thy word."

Verses 10 and 11 speak of our need of divine guidance and of the assurance that in God's Word we shall find strength to resist sin and temptation: "With my whole heart have I sought thee: O let me not wander from thy commandments. Thy word have I hid in mine heart, that I might not sin against thee."

A petition for instruction is found in verse 12: "Blessed art thou, O Lord: teach me thy statutes." In our generation when so many new truths are making claims for our allegiance, we need God's guidance and instruction. Too many are quick to accept almost any new pronouncement of science as "gospel truth," but are almost as quick to reject or ignore theological truth about which they have some question. When their television set breaks down they take it to someone who understands electronics and knows how to fix it, but when their faith breaks down they simply surrender it, without ever seeking help from someone skilled in theology or from the resources of the Word of God.

Verses 14 and 16 tell of the joy to be gleaned from the Word: "I have rejoiced in the way of thy testimonies, as much as in all riches.

. . . I will delight myself in thy statutes: I will not forget thy word."
The enthusiasm expressed in verse 97 is contagious: "O how love I
thy law!"

Our spiritual ancestors did not think of God's commandments as
being harsh and restricting regulations or as chains limiting our normal
desires of free expression. Rather, the Word brought joy and freedom.
The Bible, of course, does teach that some principles are inviolate.
They are structured into the very character of the universe. In a
sense we cannot break God's laws; we break ourselves against them
and in turn deprive ourselves of the genuine joy that is the reward
for righteous living.

A young man told me about one of his associates who had violated
minor laws and major ethical principles and was apparently "getting
by" with it. Or so he thought. Then the day came when he desperately
needed a letter of recommendation and learned to his dismay that
no one would provide it. He had wasted his credit and earned a repu-
tation for dishonesty. "You may think you can get by with shady
practices," commented my acquaintance, "but in the end what you
are catches up with you."

The Psalmist may well have known such persons, for in verses 98-
100 he writes of the treasures of wisdom and understanding which
belong to us when we come more and more to appreciate God's eternal
truths: "Thou through thy commandments hast made me wiser than
mine enemies. . . . I have more understanding than all my teachers:
for thy testimonies are my meditation. I understand more than the an-
cients, because I keep thy precepts."

Verse 105 promises that the way we travel will be illumined: "Thy
word is a lamp unto my feet, and a light unto my path." In a world
that is overshadowed by doubts and fears, we need assurance that
there is a light sufficient for our needs. That light has come! "In him
was life; and the life was the light of men" (John 1:4). Jesus said, "I
am the light of the world: he that followeth me shall not walk in darkness, but shall have the light of life" (John 8:12). Do you wonder
that the great Thomas Carlyle wrote, "In the poorest cottage are
Books: is one Book, wherein for several thousands of years the spirit
of man has found light, and nourishment, and an interpreting response
to whatever is Deepest in him"?[1]

When the Rotary Club of Emmaus, Pennsylvania, presented a

blind boy with an eighteen-volume Bible in braille, there were tears in many eyes as the men watched the lad open one of the volumes and read the Nativity Story and other familiar passages. They saw, as it were, light and life come to the boy as the Word of God became his own.

Verses 111 and 112 suggest the treasures of comfort and hope: "Thy testimonies have I taken as an heritage for ever: for they are the rejoicing of my heart. I have inclined mine heart to perform thy statutes alway, even unto the end." Elmer A. Leslie translates these verses in this manner: "Thy laws are my inheritance forever, for they are the joy of my heart. Incline my heart to perform Thy statutes; the reward lasts forever."[2]

What strength is coupled with this hope! Verse 114 is bright with assurance: "Thou art my hiding place and my shield: I hope in thy word." On the day that the Nazis invaded Norway, Bishop Berggrav says that the words found in John 14:1 were the verses stated to be read in all Lutheran churches. The courageous bishop tells us that the ordinary English translation—"Let not your heart be troubled: ye believe in God, believe also in me"—is more vigorous and direct in the Norwegian form, which reads, "Do not be in panic: believe in God, believe also in me." This verse was for them a word direct from the Lord for that dark period and gave them assurance that the day of freedom would once more dawn.

II

Lest these biblical treasures become lost treasures, let us ask, "How may the Bible mean more to each one of us?" First, we must read God's word regularly and systematically. Hit-and-miss reading will bring no lasting or life-giving power into our lives. A daily schedule for Bible reading has raised the tenor of millions of lives. Whenever we read or in whatever circumstances, we should seek to emulate Daniel of old who "kneeled upon his knees three times a day, and prayed, and gave thanks before his God" (Dan. 6:10).

Some persons prefer the practice of reading through the entire Bible, a chapter or two a day. Others find more benefit in concentrating upon and rereading the Christian witness as found in the New Testament. There are many procedures, and each is valuable. Follow the systematic pattern which meets your individual need. Most of our denominations provide prayer guides or devotional booklets. The American Bible Society circulates schedules for daily reading of the Bible.

The Bible will mean more if we not only read it, but if we study it carefully and thoughtfully. No other book has had so many books written about it. I am told that the books about the Bible which are catalogued in the Library of Congress would, if placed end to end, stretch for a distance of more than a mile! These interpretations, commentaries, and study guides, though not adequate substitutes for actual Bible reading, will help us better to understand and appreciate what we find in the Book of Books. Do not miss altogether the rich and rewarding possibilities that come from the writings of dedicated men who have given their lifelong energies to the study of God's Word.

When a young theological student showed me his bright new Bible, an ordination gift from his father, and told me that it was the only book he would need in his preaching, I showed him my well-worn Bible and shelf upon shelf of other books from which I had gleaned insight and wisdom concerning the Word.

Study the Bible and other books about it with all the discipline and persistence you can muster. Remember the Apostle's counsel: "Study to shew thyself approved unto God, a workman that needeth not to be ashamed, rightly dividing the word of truth" (2 Tim. 2:15).

It is important, furthermore, that we memorize Bible verses. Such passages will shore up our minds and hearts against the day of trouble and temptation. God's Word, hidden in our hearts, will return, like bread cast upon the waters, to bless and sustain in times of crisis and trial.

I stood at the hospital bed of a young woman who was suffering great pain. Because of her distress, she did not wish to talk. I reminded her of a verse she had long before committed to memory: "In quietness and in confidence shall be your strength" (Isa. 30:15). These were healing words. A smile came over her face, she relaxed in that quiet confidence of which the verse speaks, and she and I knew that all would be well.

We need also to demonstrate the truths of the Bible by word and deed. Other men will come to know and believe the Word when they see that we strive to live according to its precepts. Paul wrote to the Corinthians, "You yourselves are our testimonial, written in our hearts and yet open for anyone to inspect and read. You are an open letter about Christ which we ourselves have written, not with pen and ink but with the Spirit of the living God" (2 Cor. 3:2-3, PHILLIPS). The finest of all modern translations of the Bible is the translation of God's word into daily living.

> You are writing a Gospel,
>   A chapter each day,
> By deeds that you do,
>   By words that you say.
>
> Men read what you write,
>   Whether faithless or true;
> Say, what is the Gospel
>   According to You?[3]

III

The Bible will help us in times of temptation and stress. I have already quoted the words, "Thy word have I hid in mine heart, that I might not sin against thee." But the help which the Bible offers is not merely negative; it is positive as well. When "it is my meditation all the day," we are delivered from temptations and led along the paths of righteousness. Even as preventive medicines ward off sickness, so does Bible reading prevent us from stumbling unawares into sin. To read the Bible meaningfully and to apply its instruction to daily situations is the best available spiritual insurance. But the application is essential! "The man who simply hears [the Word] and does nothing about it is like a man catching the reflection of his own face in a mirror. He sees himself, it is true, but he goes on with whatever he was doing without the slightest recollection of what sort of person he saw in the mirror. But the man who looks into the perfect mirror of God's Law . . . and makes a habit of so doing, is not the man who sees and forgets" (Jas. 1:23-25, PHILLIPS).

A great building which towers high above the sidewalks rests securely on pilings driven deep into the earth. Righteous living likewise requires foundations that do not rest on shifting sands.

> How firm a foundation, ye saints of the Lord,
> Is laid for your faith in His excellent word![4]

The Bible offers the believer *revelation*. Within its pages we find revealed God and his truth. Christ is presented as the supreme revelation of the love and truth of God. To be sure, it is a progressive revelation. As we move through the Bible we read of the God of creation, the God of law and justice, the God of power, wrath, and righteousness, and the God of loving compassion and concern for his wayward children. In our search for God's revealed will we are not without assistance. "When he, the Spirit of truth, is come, he will guide you into all truth" (John 16:13). Having this assurance, the Christian knows that God's truth will minister to each of the believer's needs as they arise.

The Bible opens the door of *salvation*. Christ is God's answer to the world's sin and need. The Bible tells us that "there is none other name under heaven given among men, whereby we must be saved" (Acts 4:12). Salvation is a personal matter which awaits any man who accepts God's promise of forgiveness of sin and new life in Christ. Those who were preparing a Christmas pageant in a California migrant camp asked a young man to take a small part. He demurred, saying that he was not a believer, but when they further urged him, he said he would participate if he could understand the story of the Nativity. In a Spanish-language Bible they showed him where to read. During the following week he read page after page. When the pageant had been presented, the young migrant said to the pastor, "I want Christ to be my Savior and I wish to belong to the church." He, like so many others, had found personal salvation through faith in the living Christ revealed within the pages of the book.

The Bible also calls us to *dedication*. We must serve in our generation as others served faithfully before us. Jesus said, "I will build my church" (Matt. 16:18). Like a great Gothic cathedral, which is never complete and to which each generation must add, Christ's church is still being built. He needs our hands and he requires our talents.

> We would be building; temples still undone
> O'er crumbling walls their crosses scarcely lift;
> Waiting till love can raise the broken stone,
> And hearts creative bridge the human rift;

> We would be building, Master, let Thy plan
> Reveal the life that God would give to man.[5]

Our dedicated efforts are linked to the power of Christ to bring nearer the day when his prayer, "Thy kingdom come. Thy will be done in earth, as it is in heaven," will become a universal reality.

The Bible shows us that dedication is required but also that a *divine commission* is given to Christians. "Go ye therefore, and teach all nations, baptizing them in the name of the Father, and of the Son, and of the Holy Ghost" (Matt. 28:19). This is a command that has never been withdrawn. We are under the imperative both to give the gospel to all the world and also to relate it to every area of life. Righteousness, truth, and brotherhood are words only if they are not applied to the social conditions in which we live and to the evils of our own generation. The Bible is a goad lest we fail to pray for others, or cringe before the demands of truth, or become forgetful of our personal responsibility to serve the cause of righteousness.

The Bible provides *inspiration* for this task. Joy comes when we give ourselves to the building of a better world and a hope-filled tomorrow. But we shall soon exhaust ourselves if we do not maintain channels of communication with the Most High, who is our stimulus, our motivating force, and our undergirding strength. God's Word is our unfailing source to help us to persevere, to endure, and at last to achieve a measure of victory.

I heard Ernest Gordon, who in his book *Through the Valley of the Kwai* vividly records his experiences in a prison camp on the River Kwai, speak of what the Bible came to mean to him in that heart-wrenching situation. A lad named Jock found his place of service in the camp by passing God's Word from one group to another. Hobbling through the camp, he took Bibles from a rice sack for distribution to men who hungered for light and hope. Then he would collect them again and move on, always saying, "Here is God's Word for today." During his brief life that was his ministry—offering a divine message to despairing and dying prisoners.

When Gordon was later released and transferred to a modern hospital, the chaplain gave him a new Bible. "We needed this in the jungle," he said. "Now in our freedom we shall need it more than ever."

God's Word is our incomparable treasure, whether we are free or chained in bondage to sin, fear, or trouble. When we read it, cherish it, study it, and live it, we shall know for ourselves the meaning of these words:

> Holy Bible, book divine,
> Precious treasure, thou art mine.[6]

16.

How to Live in the Space Age

SCIENTISTS ARE TODAY AMONG our most impassioned evangelists. Time and again we hear them call for a greater awareness and use of our spiritual resources. They recognize that as we make ever greater strides in our growing command of physical forces we cannot permit our spiritual life to languish. We shall fare poorly indeed if we span the heavens at incredible speeds and move religiously at a turtle's pace.

Dr. Arthur H. Compton, Nobel physicist and devout Christian layman, said:

> Science is a reliable method of finding truth. Religion is the search for a satisfying way of life. Science is growing —yet a world that has science needs, as never before, the inspiration that religion has to offer. Beyond the nature taught by science is the Spirit that gives meaning to life.[1]

Dr. Raymond B. Fosdick, long-time president of the Rockefeller Foundation, has written, "We are discovering the right things in the wrong order, which is another way of saying that we are learning how to control nature before we have learned how to control ourselves."[2]

In the light of such comments, it is interesting to find Dr. Donald Andrews, a distinguished scientist at Johns Hopkins University, calling for "a faith for the space age."[3] Very rightly he stresses the fact that the basic answers to the problems of our day must be spiritual if the space age is to offer constructive and not destructive progress.

Within our generation two remarkable achievements have been possible through scientific know-how and genius. They are the atomic age and the space age. Each offers tremendous promise for the building of a better world—or the destruction of the world.

Now, as always, God is essential within the widening arc of man's knowledge. Listen to what a character in one of Sholem Asch's novels has to say on this very point:

The concept of divinity . . . is not a luxury; it is a necessity for man's existence, a must for his life. That is why it was molded into the very embryo of the first man. It is what we thirst for, what we search for, our driving force, our hunger for God. He exists in us, not outside of us. The further the horizon of our knowledge extends, the richer the sum of our experiences—and thus the reach of our concept—all the more will man be limited to the tiny island of his own ego, the elemental bond which binds him to his creator.[4]

In this day when space vehicles are transmitting voices from the sky, we must not forget the Voice that spoke from the heavens at the time of Jesus' baptism, saying, "This is my beloved Son, in whom I am well pleased" (Matt. 3:17), and on the occasion of the Transfiguration, "This is my beloved Son, in whom I am well pleased; hear ye him" (Matt. 17:5).

I

Our introduction into the space age did not bring, as we may have hoped, an elimination of human problems. Our moral thrust has not equaled our scientific ingenuity. Nor may we permit ourselves the delusion of thinking that science can solve soul problems with laboratory techniques.

Our lives are being lived within a complexity of conflicts. In the economic area the conflict is between socialism and free enterprise; in the political realm, between communism and democracy; in religion, between a materialistic secularism and Christianity. In many lands men are being forced to make a choice between a totalitarian control of human existence and the Christian concept of reverence for life and the supreme worth of the individual soul. Socially we are experiencing shifts in status and changing patterns of life and environment as thousands shift from rural to urban residence. Millions of others are beset with new problems as they move from being subject peoples to freedom. Tensions multiply between the "haves" and the "have-nots," the white and the colored races, and the older and the newer nations.

Such circumstances make it easy for us to lapse into an attitude of fear and insecurity and to embrace intolerant and prejudiced positions. Some people hope to retreat from reality by pretending "it isn't so" or by simply ignoring change, thinking or hoping it will go away. These persons have not learned that the "good old days" never return. Others face the new age with aggressive attitudes, preach violence and hate, and encourage bombings and disrespect for law.

This is a day when Christians, knowing that Christianity was born in a time of tension and conflict and has survived innumerable crises, should look up and take their stand on higher ground. We need the faith and resolution to believe in and work for all that Jesus anticipated when he taught us to pray for the coming of the Kingdom.

Strange new gospels and false philosophies are prepared to do battle with our hallowed revelation. I was in Berlin when Walter Ulbricht proclaimed his "Ten Commandments" for the eighteen million persons in East Germany. Previously he had proposed the substituting of Communist ceremonies for Christian baptism, confirmation, marriage, and funeral rites. His commandments are typical of the philosophy with which communism challenges Christianity.

   I. Thou shalt devote thyself to the international solidarity of the working class, all working people, and to the unbreakable alliance of the socialist nations.

  II. Thou shalt love thy fatherland and be prepared to devote all thy power and capabilities to the defense of the workers' and farmers' might.

 III. Thou shalt help eliminate the exploitation of men by men.

 IV. Thou shalt perform good deeds for socialism, knowing that socialism leads to a better life for all working people.

  V. Thou shalt perform in the spirit of mutual help in comradely collaboration for the construction of socialism, taking to heart and respecting collective criticism.

 VI. Thou shalt guard and increase the property of the people.

VII. Thou shalt strive for the improvement of thy work, be economical and strengthen socialist working discipline.

VIII. Thou shalt educate thy children in the spirit of peace and social-
      ism, steeling their character and bodily development.
  IX. Thou shalt dwell cleanly and properly, respecting thy family.
   X. Thou shalt declare thy solidarity with the peoples fighting for na-
      tional liberation and national independence.

To this Mr. Ulbricht adds: "These are the commandments for our
new socialist ethic and a firm part of our world outlook."

How discordant the words of this twentieth-century heresy sound
when contrasted with God's pronouncement from Mount Sinai and
especially with the proclamation of Jesus: "The first of all the commandments is, Hear, O Israel; The Lord our God is one Lord: and
thou shalt love the Lord thy God with all thy heart, and with all thy
soul, and with all thy mind, and with all thy strength: this is the first
commandment. And the second is like, namely this, Thou shalt love
thy neighbor as thyself. There is none other commandment greater
than these" (Mark 12:29-31).

                                    II

There are certain affirmations which we as Christians must stress if
our faith is to prove adequate for the space age. These affirmations
center in Christ our Lord and the way of life he taught.

First, a faith for the space age calls for an emphasis on the *truth*.
By truth I mean the Christian truth as we find it in God's Word and
in him who said, "I am . . . the truth" (John 14:6). Here we find
assurance of salvation from personal sin through faith in Christ as
Lord and a basis for social righteousness and world redemption.

An adequate faith for our day requires spiritual power that enables
us to use aright the physical powers that surround us. Someone has
well said, "Protons, neutrons, and electrons cannot be entrusted to
spiritual morons." God's truth will make us free to use these new
powers for his glory, for we have the promise, "As many as received
him, to them gave he power to become the sons of God, even to them
that believe on his name" (John 1:12). This power bestows the truth
that "shall make you free" (John 8:32).

Secondly, a faith for the space age calls for *trained minds*. Democracy calls for an intelligent and educated electorate. The hazards and
hopes of atomic inventiveness and space-age daring rest with enlight-

ened minds, intelligent leaders, and educated peoples. We shall never solve our problems by closing our public schools or by educating only those who can afford it. Henry Cook has wisely said, "Minds determine history."

Christian education is not an elective in the curriculum of life. Paul wrote to young Timothy, "God hath not given us the spirit of fear; but . . . of a sound mind" (2 Tim. 1:7). Christians have always believed that the mind is a priceless gift from God to be treasured, nurtured, and guided in ways that will honor and glorify the Eternal. This truth is evidenced in a book entitled *Christian Prayers,* published in 1578, which includes this petition:

O God, who art nigh to all them that call upon thee in truth; who art thyself the Truth, whom to know is perfect knowledge: instruct us with thy divine wisdom, and teach us thy law; that we may know the truth and walk in it; through him in whom the truth was made manifest, even Jesus Christ thy Son our Lord. Amen.

In his name and for his sake Christians have built schools, established libraries, published books, and dispatched ambassadors of enlightenment to every crossroad, even unto the ends of the earth. No body of men has equaled Christians in the initiation and promulgation of educational endeavor. And our labors are not complete.

> O grant us light, that we may see
> Where error lurks in human lore,
> And turn our seeking minds to Thee,
> And love Thy holy Word the more.[5]

More than a century ago Daniel Webster uttered words which still mirror our dedication to all that trains the mind:

If we work upon marble, it will perish. If we work upon brass, time will efface it. If we rear temples, they will crumble to dust. But if we work upon men's immortal minds, if we imbue them with high principles, with the just fear of God and love of their fellow men, we engrave on those tablets something which no time can efface, and which will brighten and brighten to all eternity.[6]

In any final reckoning the course of history is determined not by the Alexanders, Caesars, Napoleons, and Hitlers, but by the minds of men like Socrates, Moses, Paul, Augustine, Calvin, and—towering above all—Jesus. How we need the mind of Christ in our day and generation!

Thirdly, a faith for the space age calls for *Christian morality*. Honesty, integrity, and purity of mind and purpose are not desirable luxuries; they are minimal necessities.

We need to take to task the threat to Christlike behavior represented in these words by a character in a twentieth-century novel:

Living modernly's living quickly. . . . You can't cart a wagon-load of ideals and romanticisms with you these days. When you travel by airplane, you must leave your heavy baggage behind. The good old-fashioned soul was all right when people lived slowly. But it's too ponderous nowadays. There's no room for it in the airplane.[7]

These words remind me of what Mark Twain said: "Human beings are the only creatures that can blush—and that need to."

The space age needs desperately a new commitment to the old-fashioned—and never out-of-date—fruits of the spirit such as love, joy, meekness, gentleness, and self-control.

Fourthly, a faith for the space age calls for the proclaiming of *peace* in the name of the Prince of Peace. Within our generation the world has become a neighborhood. We live in everyone's backyard, so to speak, and our voices can be thrown across any fences. The conquering of space has put everyone at our elbow.

The inscription on the tombstone of Captain Freeman Hatch in Evergreen Cemetery, Eastham, Massachusetts, illustrates vividly how considerably shrunken our world has become within the past century.

> In 1852 he became famous making the
> astonishing passage in Clipper
> Ship Northern Light from San
> Francisco to Boston
> in 76 days 6 hours
> an achivement won by no
> mortal before or since.[8]

But our scientific achievements will be only hollow victories unless this new neighborhood is transformed into a brotherhood by our practice of love, kindness, sympathy, and consideration. Every Christian must be a Samaritan on the Jericho road all humanity travels. Jesus was right when he said that peace was the accomplishment, not of military prowess, but of redeemed hearts. "Blessed are the peacemakers" (Matt. 5:9).

III

We who believe in the supremacy of Christ as Savior and Lord have much to contribute to space-age living. God charges us with the responsibility to call men to a new devotion to the Word of God, our sole and sufficient authority for faith and practice. Our obligation is to proclaim that "the Word was made flesh, and dwelt among us" (John 1:14). We know that no man, home, or nation remains the same when Jesus is welcomed. We accomplish our purpose through evangelism and missions as with love and truth we train minds in faith and morality and the ways of peace.

A young pastor of an overseas church told me of an older man who came to him at the close of a service and asked, "Is what you preached today really true?"

The young pastor said, "Yes, of course, it is true. It comes from the Word of God."

The older man urged him further, "Then lead me to God."

A little later the two held a conference in which they talked about Christ and the way of salvation. At the end the pastor said, "Let's talk with God."

"I don't know how," the older man protested.

The pastor counseled, "Talk with him just as you have talked with me."

On the following day the older man returned, saying, "On the way home I talked with God." Then with a light shining in his eyes, he added, "After a while peace and joy came to my heart. I want everyone to know what Jesus means to me."

This simple experience sounds like a page from the Book of Acts, and in a sense it is, for the Spirit which changed men's lives long ago still brings the Good News—the Best News—of the Gospel. The Living Christ is our answer to the problems and challenges of space-age living.

Notes

1. *Please Tell Me How . . .*

1. From "What Is Prayer?" by James Montgomery.
2. From "Prayer" by Richard Chenevix Trench.
3. From "The Rime of the Ancient Mariner" by Samuel T. Coleridge.
4. From *Worship Resources for the Christian Year,* ed. by Charles L. Wallis (New York: Harper & Row, 1954). Reprinted by permission.
5. From "Song" by Louis Ginsberg.
6. Margaret Lee Runbeck, *Hope of Earth* (Boston: Houghton Mifflin Co.), p. 452.
7. From "On His Blindness" by John Milton.
8. Rumer Godden, *An Episode of Sparrows* (New York: The Viking Press, Inc.), p. 208.

2. *How to Face Up to Life*

1. Edith Deen, *All of the Women of the Bible* (New York: Harper & Row, 1955), p. 126.
2. Ralph Waldo Emerson, *Essays* ("Gifts").
3. "Thanks Be to God" by Janie Alford. Reprinted from *Masterpeices of Religious Verse,* ed. by James Dalton Morrison (New York: Harper & Row, 1948).
4. "As a Man Soweth" by Johann Wolfgang von Goethe.
5. From hymn by Horatius Bonar.

3. *How to Look at Yourself*

1. From "To a Louse" by Robert Burns.
2. Lloyd C. Douglas, *The Robe* (Boston: Houghton Mifflin Co., 1942), Chapter XVII.
3. "The Ways" by John Oxenham. Reprinted by permission from *Selected Poems of John Oxenham* (New York: Harper & Row, 1948).

4. *How to Become More Than You Are*

1. "Some Faith at Any Cost" by Harriet du Autermont. Reprinted from *Masterpieces of Religious Verse,* ed. by James Dalton Morrison (New York: Harper & Row, 1948).
2. John Steinbeck, *The Grapes of Wrath* (New York: The Viking Press, 1939), p. 204.
3. Romain Rolland, *Jean-Christophe,* tr. by Gilbert Canaan (New York: Holt, Rinehart & Winston, Inc., 1910), p. 232.

5. *How to Be Good and Good for Something*

1. From "Myself" by Edgar A. Guest. Reprinted by permission from *Collected Verse of Edgar A. Guest* (Chicago: Reilly & Lee Co., 1934).
2. William Shakespeare, *Hamlet* (Act I).
3. Rumer Godden, *The River* (Boston: Little, Brown & Co., Inc., 1946), pp. 137 f.
4. Source unknown.
5. "Stubborn Ounces" by Bonaro W. Overstreet. Reprinted by permission from *Hands Laid upon the Wind* by Bonaro W. Overstreet (New York: W. W. Norton & Co., Inc., 1955).
6. Eve Curie, *Madame Curie* (Garden City: Doubleday & Co., 1937), p. 158.
7. John Galsworthy, *Maid in Waiting* (New York: Charles Scribner's Sons, 1931), pp. 235 f. Reprinted by permission.
8. Lenore Coffee and William Joyce Cowen, *Family Portrait* (New York: Samuel French, Inc., 1940), pp. 127 f. Copyright by Lenore Coffee and William Joyce Cowen. Reprinted by permission of the authors.

6. *How to Be Like a Tree*

1. From "Trees" by Joyce Kilmer. *Trees and Other Poems* by Joyce Kilmer (Garden City: Doubleday & Co., 1914).
2. From "Speech at the Diet of Worms."
3. From "The Marshes of Glynn" by Sidney Lanier.

7. *How to Practice What You Preach*

1. William Shakespeare, *The Merchant of Venice* (Act I, sc. 2).
2. "Dreams and Deeds" by John Hunter.
3. From "Laborare est Orare" by Frances A. R. Russell.
4. Source unknown.
5. From hymn by Philip Doddridge.

8. *How to Know the Supreme Fact in Life*

1. From hymn by Matthew Bridges.
2. From hymn by John Bowring.
3. From *The Gauntlet* by James Street. Copyright 1945 by James Street. Reprinted by permission of Doubleday & Company, Inc.
4. From hymn by Edward Mote.
5. Christopher Fry, *A Sleep of Prisoners* (New York: Oxford University Press, 1951), p. 13.
6. "Searching after God" by Thomas Heywood.
7. From "The Unknown God" by William Watson. Reprinted from *The Poems of Sir William Watson, 1878-1935,* by permission of George G. Harrap & Co., Ltd.
8. John Galsworthy, *In Chancery* in *The Forsyte Saga* (Modern Standard Authors Series; New York: Charles Scribner's Sons, 1920), II, 313. Used by permission of the publisher.
9. From hymn by Phillips Brooks.
10. From "The Crystal" by Sidney Lanier.

9. *How to Live a New Kind of Life*

1. Elisabeth Elliott, *The Savage My Kinsman* (New York: Harper & Row, 1961), p. 94.
2. H. G. Wells, *Mr. Britling Sees It Through* (New York: The Macmillan Company, 1916), p. 442.
3. From hymn by R. H. McDaniel.
4. From "O World" by George Santayana. Reprinted from *Poems* by George Santayana, copyright 1921, by permission of Charles Scribner's Sons.
5. From "The Eternal Goodness" by John Greenleaf Whittier.
6. From hymn by Colin Sterne.
7. From letter to Thurlow Weed, March 14, 1865.
8. From "The Chambered Nautilus" by Oliver Wendell Holmes.
9. George Bernard Shaw, *Androcles and the Lion* (Act III) (New York: Dodd, Mead & Co., 1941).
10. From "Foreign Missions in Battle Array" by Vachel Lindsay.
11. Maxwell Anderson, *Valley Forge* (Act III), in *Eleven Verse Plays* by Maxwell Anderson (New York. Harcourt, Brace & World, Inc., 1940).

12. Source unknown.
13. Elliott, *op. cit.*, p. 159.

10. *How to Become a Better Christian*

1. From "Andrea del Sarto" by Robert Browning.
2. Victor Hugo, *Les Misérables*.
3. Author unknown. Reprinted from *A Treasury of Poems for Worship and Devotion,* ed. by Charles L. Wallis (New York: Harper & Row, 1959).
4. From "Trial by Ice," *Life,* July 9, 1951. Quoted in *Preaching* by Walter Russell Bowie, p. 158.
5. Maurice Herzog, *Annapurna* (New York: E. P. Dutton & Co., 1953). Quoted in *ibid*.
6. Story related to author by Roy Angell.

11. *How to Be Found Faithful with Life*

1. "The Pilgrim Way" by John Oxenham. Reprinted by permission from *Selected Poems of John Oxenham* (New York: Harper & Row, 1948).
2. From hymn by Samuel Longfellow.
3. From "The Brewing of Soma" by John Greenleaf Whittier.
4. From hymn by Samuel F. Stone.
5. William Shakespeare, *Hamlet* (Act III, sc. 1).
6. From hymn by Harry Emerson Fosdick. Used with permission of the author.
7. From hymn by Frank Mason North.

12. *How to Live in Peace*

1. "The Place of Peace" by Edwin Markham. Reprinted by permission from *Poems of Edwin Markham* (New York: Harper & Row, 1950).
2. A. J. Cronin, *The Keys of the Kingdom* (Boston: Little, Brown & Co., Inc., 1941), p. 320.

13. *How the Lord Helps Those Who Help Themselves*

1. George Moore, *Aphrodite in Aulis,* p. 28.
2. George Macdonald, *The Marquis of Lossie,* Chap. 27.
3. Miguel de Unamuno, *The Tragic Sense of Life*.
4. From *In Memoriam* by Alfred Tennyson.
5. From "The Pillar of the Cloud" by John Henry Newman.

6. Mary Ellen Chase, *The Lovely Ambition* (New York: W. W. Norton & Co., Inc., 1960), p. 210.
7. Graham Greene, *The End of the Affair* (New York: The Viking Press, 1951), pp. 146 f.
8. From hymn by Frances R. Havergal.

14. *How Prayer Can Mean More to You*

1. From *In Memoriam* by Alfred Tennyson.
2. Johannes Kepler, *When Studying Astronomy*.
3. Marc Connelly, *The Green Pastures* (New York: Holt, Rinehart & Winston, Inc., 1960), p. 144.
4. From hymn by Frances R. Havergal.
5. Martin Luther, *Table Talk* ("Of Prayer").
6. From hymn by William D. Longstaff.
7. From "Morte d'Arthur" by Alfred Tennyson.
8. Lloyd C. Douglas, *The Big Fisherman* (Boston: Houghton Mifflin Co., 1948), pp. 106 f.
9. From untitled poem by Marion Franklin Ham.
10. From *Aurora Leigh* by Elizabeth Barrett Browning.
11. From hymn by Johnson Oatman.
12. From "Morte d'Arthur" by Alfred Tennyson.
13. Archibald MacLeish, *J.B.* (Boston: Houghton Mifflin Co., 1958), p. 12. Reprinted by permission.

15. *How the Bible Can Mean More to You*

1. Thomas Carlyle, *Essays* ("Corn-Law Rhymes").
2. Elmer A. Leslie, *The Psalms* (New York: Abingdon Press, 1949), p. 181.
3. "Your Own Version" by Paul Gilbert. Reprinted from *Masterpieces of Religious Verse,* ed. James Dalton Morrison (New York: Harper & Row, 1948).
4. From Hymn "K" in Rippon's Selection.
5. From "Builders" by Purd E. Deitz. Reprinted by permission of the Board of Christian Education, The United Presbyterian Church in the U.S.A.
6. From hymn by John Burton.

16. *How to Live in the Space Age*

1. Quoted in E. Paul Hovey, ed., *The Treasury for Special Days and Occasions* (Westwood, N. J.: Fleming H. Revell Co., 1961).
2. Quoted in Gerald Kennedy, ed., *A Reader's Notebook* (New York: Harper & Row, 1953).
3. Title of article in *The Rotarian,* August, 1958, pp. 8 f.

4. Sholem Asch, *East River* (New York: G. P. Putnam's Sons, 1946), pp. 259 f. Copyright 1946 by Sholem Asch. Used by permission of the publisher.

5. From hymn by Lawrence Tuttieth.

6. From speech at Faneuil Hall, 1852.

7. Aldous Huxley, *Point Counter Point* (Garden City: Doubleday & Co., Inc., 1938), p. 242.

8. From *Stories on Stone: A Book of American Epitaphs*, ed. by Charles L. Wallis (New York: Oxford University Press, 1954), p. 40. Reprinted by permission.

Format by Mort Perry
Set in Linotype Times Roman
Composed, printed and bound by The Haddon Craftsmen, Inc.
HARPER & ROW, PUBLISHERS, INCORPORATED